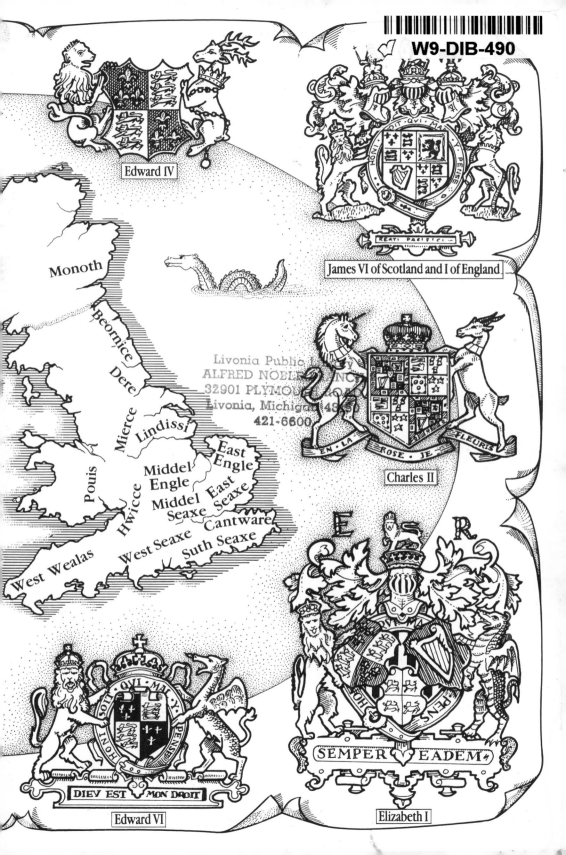

Edward IV

James VI of Scotland and I of England

Monoth

Beornice

Dere

Mierce

Lindissi

Pouis

Hwicce

Middel Engle

Middel Seaxe

East Engle

East Seaxe

West Seaxe

Cantware

West Wealas

Suth Seaxe

Charles II

Edward VI

DIEV EST MON DROIT

Elizabeth I

SEMPER ☙ EADEM

KINGS & QUEENS
of England & Great Britain

4

942.009 Delderfield, Eric R.
D   Kings & queens of England & Great Britain /
         Eric R. Delderfield ; with additional
         material by Anthony J. Lambert. -- New York :
         Facts on File, c1990.

             191 p. : ill.

             ISBN 0-8160-2433-2: $24.95   30126

                                               NOV 90

             1. Great Britain--Kings and rulers--
         Biography. 2. Anglo-Saxons--Kings and rulers
         --Biography. 3. Great Britain--History. 4.
         Anglo-Saxons--History.   I. Title.

                                                    89-25905

KINGS & QUEENS
of England & Great Britain

ERIC R. DELDERFIELD

With additional material by
ANTHONY J. LAMBERT

New York • Oxford • Sydney

ACKNOWLEDGEMENTS

The illustrations in this book are reproduced by kind permission of the following: Hulton Picture Library (pages 114, 127, 132, 139, 143, 148, 152, 155), The Mansell Collection (pages 129 and 137), The National Trust Photographic Library, photographer Bryan S. Evans (page 83), The Telegraph Colour Library (pages 159, 162, 163, 166, 167, 170, 178) and the Tim Graham Picture Library (pages 171, 174, 175, 178, 179, 183). All the remaining illustrations are reproduced by courtesy of the National Portrait Gallery, London. The genealogical trees and maps (of Saxon England and Modern Britain) were designed and drawn by Ethan Danielson, EDANART.

Library of Congress Cataloging-in-Publication Data
Delderfield, Eric R. (Eric Raymond)
Kings and Queens of England and Great Britain.
Includes bibliographical references.
1. Great Britain – Kings and rulers – Biography.
2. Anglo-Saxons – Kings and rulers – Biography.
I. Title.
DA28.1.D42   1989   942′.009′92 [B]   89-25905
ISBN 0-81602433-2

KINGS AND QUEENS OF ENGLAND AND GREAT BRITAIN is published for the first time in 1990 and is based on the work of Eric Delderfield and Anthony Lambert. Much of the text and all of the colour illustrations are new but some text material has been drawn from earlier works by Eric Delderfield.

Facts on File, Inc.
460 Park Avenue South
New York NY 10016

Typeset in Garamond ITC by
ABM Typographics Limited, Hull, England.
and printed in West Germany
by Mohndruck Gmbh.

10 9 8 7 6 5 4 3 2 1

This book is printed on acid-free paper.

CONTENTS

LIST OF ILLUSTRATIONS

THE DYNASTIES

There have been about sixty-six monarchs of England spread over a period of about 1,150 years. These men and women have represented the following dynasties:

Saxons

Normans

Plantagenets

House of Lancaster

House of York

Tudors

Stuarts

Hanoverians

Saxe-Coburgs

Windsors

PART ONE

SAXONS, NORMANS,

PLANTAGENETS

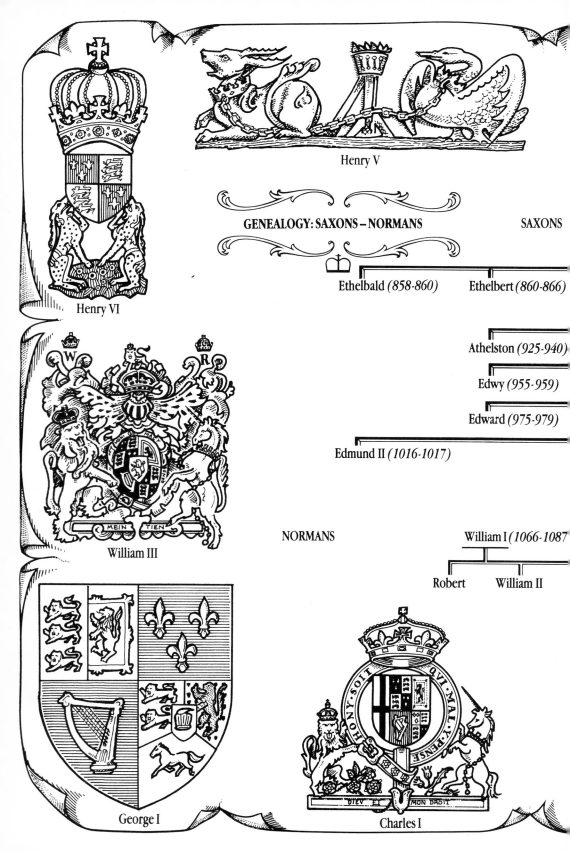

Henry V

GENEALOGY: SAXONS – NORMANS

SAXONS

Henry VI

Ethelbald *(858-860)*

Ethelbert *(860-866)*

Athelston *(925-940)*

Edwy *(955-959)*

Edward *(975-979)*

Edmund II *(1016-1017)*

William III

NORMANS

William I *(1066-1087)*

Robert

William II

George I

Charles I

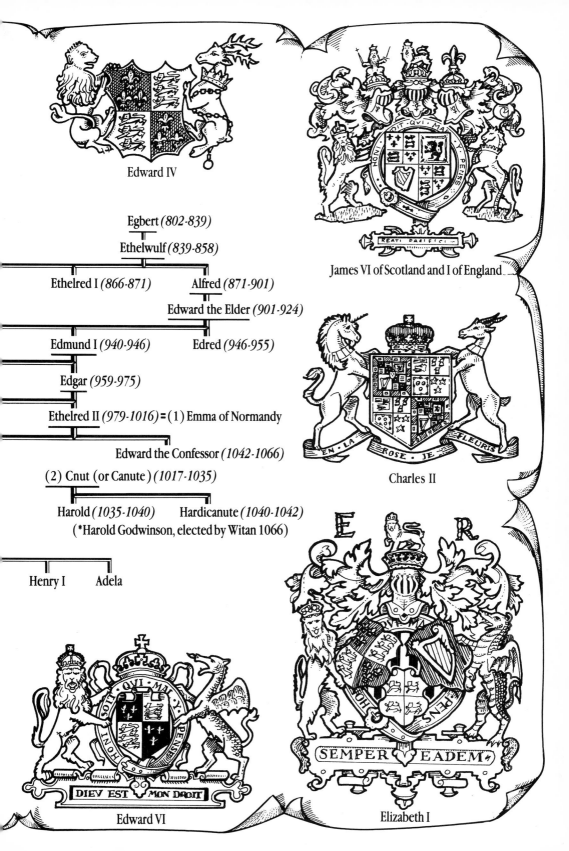

Edward IV

James VI of Scotland and I of England

Egbert *(802-839)*

Ethelwulf *(839-858)*

Ethelred I *(866-871)*   Alfred *(871-901)*

Edward the Elder *(901-924)*

Edmund I *(940-946)*   Edred *(946-955)*

Edgar *(959-975)*

Ethelred II *(979-1016)* = (1) Emma of Normandy

Edward the Confessor *(1042-1066)*

(2) Cnut (or Canute) *(1017-1035)*

Charles II

Harold *(1035-1040)*   Hardicanute *(1040-1042)*
(*Harold Godwinson, elected by Witan 1066)

Henry I   Adela

Edward VI

Elizabeth I

PRE-CONQUEST KINGS

Saxon Kings

EGBERT: ascended throne 802. Reigned 37 years. Died 839.

ETHELWULF: ascended throne 839. Reigned 19 years. (Son of Egbert.) Died 858. Buried Winchester.

ETHELBALD: ascended throne 858. Reigned 2 years. (2nd son of Ethelwulf. Married father's widow.) Died 860. Buried Sherborne.

ETHELBERT: ascended throne 860. Reigned 6 years. (3rd son of Ethelwulf.) Died 866. Buried Sherborne.

ST ETHELRED I: ascended throne 866. Reigned 5 years. (4th son of Ethelwulf.) Died 871. Buried Wimborne.

ALFRED: born c.848. Ascended throne 871. Reigned 28 years. (5th son of Ethelwulf.) Died 899, aged 51. Buried Winchester.

EDWARD THE ELDER: ascended throne 899. Reigned 26 years. (Son of Alfred.) Died 925. Buried Winchester.

ATHELSTAN: born 895. Ascended throne 925. Reigned 14 years. Died 939. Buried Malmesbury.

EDMUND I: born ?922. Ascended throne 939. Reigned 7 years. Died 946 (assassinated). Buried Glastonbury.

EADRED: ascended throne 946. Reigned 9 years. Died 955. Buried Winchester.

EDWY: born 940. Ascended throne 955. Reigned 4 years. Died 959, aged 19. Buried Winchester.

EDGAR: born 944. Ascended throne 959. Reigned 16 years. Died 975, aged 31. Buried Glastonbury.

EDWARD THE MARTYR: born c.962. Ascended throne 975. Reigned 4 years. Died 978, aged 16 (assassinated). Buried (i) Wareham (ii) Shaftesbury.

ETHELRED II: born ?968. Ascended throne 978. Reigned 38 years. Died 1016, aged 48. Buried St Paul's, London.

EDMUND II: born ?988. Ascended throne 1016. Reigned 6 months. Died 1016, aged 47. Buried St Paul's, London.

EDWARD THE CONFESSOR: born c.1002-1007. Ascended throne 1042. Reigned 24 years. Died 1066. Buried Westminster Abbey, London.

HAROLD II: born ?1022. Ascended throne 1066. (Brother-in-law of Edward the Confessor.) Reigned 10 months. Died 1066, aged ?44. Burial place unknown, possibly Waltham Abbey.

Danish Kings

CNUT (or **CANUTE**): born c.995. Ascended throne 1016. Reigned 19 years. Died 1035, aged 40. Buried Winchester.
HAROLD I: born 1017. Ascended throne 1035. Reigned 5 years. Died 1040, aged 23. Buried St Clement Danes, London.
HARTHACNUT: born 1018. Ascended throne 1040. Reigned 2 years. Died 1042, aged 24. Buried Winchester.

Saxon Kings

The Roman occupation of England left surprisingly little mark on the future. In France and Spain the effects of centuries of rule from Rome were of much greater significance: the very language of these countries is descended from the tongue of their conquerors. But in Britain most of what the Romans did perished or fell into disuse after they left. The Kingdom's language and institutions are Saxon. It is therefore with the Saxons that the continuous history of England begins.

The onset of invasion by Angles, Saxons and Jutes, sea-rovers from the shores of Germany and Frisia, began about the middle of the fourth century. The Saxon conquest of England was completed within the course of the next century and a half. As bands of Saxons settled in England, so 'Kings' became general. The word itself, 'Cyning', is probably connected with 'kin', indicating that the man stood at the head of his kindred or tribe. Kings were, then, mere tribal chieftains in origin.

By about AD 600 ten separate, but not necessarily independent kingdoms, had been established, the majority south of the Humber. The importance of seven of these kingdoms – Wessex, Sussex, Kent, Essex, East Anglia, Mercia and Northumbria – has given to the next two centuries the title of the Heptarchy.

Gradually three of the seven – Wessex, Mercia and Northumbria – began to establish some sort of domination over their smaller neighbours. Although the supremacy of individual kingdoms was usually short-lived, yet the very fact that from the late sixth century to the early ninth century they were at least subject to one common overlord, was an important influence in achieving the eventual unity of England.

Another vital factor making for unity was the appearance of Christianity in England in AD 597. Thereafter the spread of Christianity and changes of overlordship follow almost the same course. Following the death in 616 of the King of Kent, supremacy passed, along with Christianity, to Northumbria until about 685.

Mercia, which had also put aside heathen practices, filled the position left by the decline of Northumbria, almost until the end of the eighth century. But the death in 796 of Offa, perhaps the greatest of all Saxon kings save Alfred, was followed by another southerly shift of political power.

First King of England

At the battle of Ellandun, thought to have been near Winchester, in 825, Mercia's supremacy was broken by **EGBERT**, 802–839, King of Wessex. Mercia was temporarily annexed in 828 and Egbert's lordship recognized by Northumbria, prompting some historians to claim that Egbert may be regarded as the first King of England, though he did not assume that style. But his hold over the vassal kingdoms was tentative: no garrisoned forts or standing armies secured his position in them, and it took only a year for Wiglaf, King of Mercia, 827–838, to reassert Mercian independence.

The lack of any developed institutions or structure made the personal qualities of the king of paramount importance. It was the threat from across the North Sea that was to test the leadership and resilience of Saxon kings; all but the West Saxon kings were to be found wanting. The first Viking raid occurred towards the end of the eighth century, landing on the coast of Wessex, though it was not until 866 that the Viking incursions began that would bring the kingdoms of Northumbria, East Anglia and Mercia to their knees. Only Wessex stood between the Vikings and the total conquest of England; it was due to the determination of Egbert's grandsons and successive kings of Wessex that they were foiled in this objective.

Previous efforts to unite England had failed because as soon as one kingdom became great it was in the interest of the rest to pull it down. England lacked the strongest possible motive towards union, namely the presence of a foreign foe. As the West Saxon kings evicted the Danes from the other Anglo-Saxon kingdoms, their extended power brought in prospect a single king ruling over a united England.

West Saxon Kings

The outline story of the Saxon kings which follows is, then, the story of the West Saxon kings. The period from Egbert to Edgar, covering the best part of two centuries, was the golden age of the Saxon monarchy. But the next ninety years or so, to the time of the Norman Conquest, bring the story of one calamity after another: of the inability of the later Saxon kings to preserve England from Danish ravages; of the accession of weak kings like Ethelred and Edward the Confessor; and finally of the Norman Conquest itself.

Egbert died in 839, leaving a son **ETHELWULF,** 839–858. (His reign is chiefly known for the periods of bad weather connected with the name of his saintly advisor, Swithun.) He left behind him four sons: **ETHELBALD**, 858–860; **ETHELBERT**, 860–866; **ETHELRED I**, 866–871; and **ALFRED**, 871–899.

ALFRED OF WESSEX, perhaps the most famous of all England's kings, was born in 849 at Wantage in Berkshire and taken to Rome in 853. He came to the throne in 871.

The Danes had become settlers in eastern England during the middle of the ninth century, had conquered most of England and were pushing southwards into Wessex. In 871 the West Saxons fought nine battles against the Danes, at all of which Alfred was second-in-command. In the middle of the year his elder brother, Ethelred I, died. The twenty-two-year-old Alfred had won the confidence of the army and he was chosen king by the Witan (the council of the Anglo-Saxon kings). The victory at Ashdown, fought just before Alfred's accession, provided some respite from Viking incursions, but in 878 came the major crisis of his life. Guthrum, king of the Danes of East Anglia, burst into Wessex in mid-winter, compelling Alfred to seek refuge amidst the island fastnesses of the Somerset marshes. Having established a stronghold at Athelney, Alfred marshalled his forces, summoning the thegns of Wiltshire and Hampshire to rejoin his banner. It was while Alfred was at Athelney that he is said to have 'burned the cakes'. A Danish force landed at Alfred's rear and was defeated by the thegns of Devon, and in May 878 Alfred emerged to defeat the Danes at Edington in Wiltshire. In one of the pivotal battles in English history, Alfred prevented the Viking domination of England, winning such a victory that at the peace of Wedmore, Guthrum agreed to be christened.

For the next decade Alfred consolidated his hold over Wessex, created a navy and sent a fleet against the Danes of East Anglia in 884, taking London in 886. A treaty with Guthrum fixed Watling Street, the Great Ouse and the River Lea from its source as the southern boundary of Danelaw, leaving London to the English king. A period of respite enabled Alfred to turn his attention to the arts of peace, for which he showed as much aptitude as his martial skills. Alfred's varied accomplishments have led to the comparison with Charlemagne, whose scale of operation may have been larger but who never forged a united and permanent kingdom as did Alfred and his descendants.

Alfred created many fortified towns, some on old Roman sites, some on new ones; in all he founded some twenty-five towns, or about one-third the number founded by the Romans in three and a half centuries. Viking raids had destroyed libraries and even disrupted the passing on of religious knowledge and forms, leaving a clergy that no longer understood the meaning of the Latin mass they sang. He set aside a half of all revenue to be spent on educational needs; established schools where the sons of the nobility could be taught to read and write; brought in foreign scholars and craftsmen; restored monasteries and convents. He helped to design houses, invented a candle clock, mastered Latin and translated many books into Anglo-Saxon, including Boethius' *Consolation of Philosophy* and histories of Bede and Orosius. He ordered the compilation of the first English history book, the *Anglo-Saxon Chronicle*, which was continued for more than two centuries after his death. He published a collection of laws and enforced them, so that when troubles came after his death, 'men longed for the laws of King Alfred'. Had Alfred never fought a battle, he would still deserve a place among the greatest rulers of history.

Alfred the Great died in 899. The next three generations of kings were, with one exception, strong in the tradition of Alfred.

EDWARD THE ELDER, 899–925, son of Alfred, continued the work of his father and began the reconquest of Danelaw. In 910 he defeated the Danes of Northumbria at Tettenhall in Staffordshire, and spent much of the next decade struggling to clear them from Lincoln, Derby, Nottingham, Stamford and Leicester. Forts to secure the English frontier were built by Edward at Rhuddlan, Thelwall and Manchester. By the end of his reign he exercised authority over all Danish lands as far north as the Humber. A permanent union with Mercia was established in 918–19 and he developed an administrative framework for the kingdom of England. In this respect Edward the Elder is the first monarch who may be justly described as King of England. Though twice married, Edward's eldest son and successor was born of a mistress.

ATHELSTAN, 924–939, was crowned King of the West Saxons and Mercians at Kingston-upon-Thames in 924. He never lost a battle, conquering part of Cornwall, Wales and Northumbria and defeating an alliance of Welsh, Scots and Danes at Brunanburh in 937. He was the first king to have extensive contact with foreign monarchs, on religious and cultural matters as well as the negotiation of royal marriages. His religious devotion expressed itself in collecting quantities of relics and in neither marrying nor fathering any children. After a tireless life, he chose to be the first and last monarch to be buried at Malmesbury in Wiltshire, in preference to the usual mausoleum at Winchester.

Athelstan was succeeded by his half-brother, **EDMUND I**, 939–946, who further eroded Danelaw, reconquering Danish Mercia in 944. He also overran the kingdom of St Strathclyde and Cumbria before being killed by an outlaw at Pucklechurch in Gloucestershire. Edmund's brother **EADRED**, 946–955, succeeded him, and is best remembered for his defeat of a challenge to West Saxon supremacy from Eric Bloodaxe, King of York, who attempted to rid Northumbria of southern dominance. Expelled by Eadred in 948, Eric returned to fight for Northumbrian independence, but was again defeated, at Stainmore in 954. By the end of his reign Eadred was king of all England.

Eadred's nephew **EDWY** (or **EADWIG**), 955–959, accomplished little, being only fifteen when he ascended the throne. His reign was marked by his animosity towards his uncle's treasurer, Dunstan, whom he banished; Dunstan was later to become Archbishop of Canterbury during the reign of Edgar. A measure of the lack of confidence in which Edwy was held is given by the Northumbrians and Mercians renouncing their allegiance to him in favour of his brother **EDGAR**, 959–975. Known as 'The Peaceable', Edgar's reign was spared Viking invasions, and he even began to employ Danish subjects. His policy was shaped by Dunstan whose respected position helped Edgar's reputation amongst European rulers. New elements in monastic pageantry were introduced by him, his coronation at Bath emulating that of his kinsman, Otto the Great, as German emperor. Edgar's Queen, Aelfthryth, was annointed at his side, recognizing the growing political role played by English queens. When seven British, Scottish and Welsh kings came to Chester to submit formally to Edgar, they purportedly rowed him on the River Dee. Though almost certainly apocryphal, the story reflects the dominance of the erstwhile West Saxon kings.

The story of Saxon downfall begins ominously with the murder of **EDWARD THE MARTYR**, 975–978. The son of Edgar, Edward encountered opposition to his claim to the throne from supporters of his younger half-brother Aethelred. It was while visiting Aethelred at Corfe Castle in Dorset that Edward was murdered; his step-mother, Aelfthryth, is suspected of having a hand in the affair so that her favoured son **AETHELRED II 'THE UNREADY'** ('devoid of foresight'), 978–1016, could become king. His reign was beset by a renewal of Viking raids, of a ferocity unknown since Alfred's time. Powerless to defeat the invaders, Aethelred resorted to buying off the Danes with silver (Danegeld) which only encouraged further raids. On St Brice's Day, 13 November 1002, he ordered the massacre of Danes resident in England, a treachery prompting a retaliatory invasion of 1003 under Sweyn, son of the Danish king. Sweyn's military successes so eroded support for Aethelred that he could no longer rely upon the nobility or the army, compelling him to flee to Normandy in 1013. (In 1002 he had established the first link with Normandy by marrying Duke Richard's daughter Emma.) Sweyn's death in 1014 enabled Aethelred to return, but he was deprived of half the kingdom by his son Edmund who made himself ruler in Danelaw.

On the death of his father in London in 1016, **EDMUND IRONSIDE**, 1016, was chosen king by the Londoners. The Witan in Southampton had other ideas and elected a Dane, Cnut, the son of Sweyn. After a series of battles, and despite the victory of Cnut at Ashingdon in Essex, a compromise was reached whereby Cnut would rule Mercia and Northumbria, while Edmund would hold Wessex; the survivor would succeed to the whole. Cnut did not have to wait long; within a few weeks Edmund was dead, and his sons had fled to Hungary.

After a brutal start to his reign, **CNUT** (or **CANUTE**), 1016–1035, developed into a temperate and devout ruler who adopted English ideas, gradually replaced Danish earls with native Englishmen and married Emma, the widow of Aethelred. His only military campaign was in Scotland where, despite a Scots' victory at Carham in 1018, he compelled the Scottish king to submit. His support for monasteries and churches was reflected in his pilgrimage to Rome in 1027-8, which strengthened ties with the Pope. The famous story related by Henry of Huntingdon about the king getting his feet wet was reputedly an aspect of his Christian humility, to demonstrate to his sycophantic nobles that even he could not halt the waves. Towards the end of his reign he alienated his links with Scandinavia, and his choice of Winchester as a final resting place confirmed his sense of identity with the country whose monarchy he had replaced.

The illegitimate elder son of Cnut, **HAROLD I**, 1035–1040, exploited the preoccupation of his half-brother, Harthacnut, with affairs in Denmark to seize the throne that Cnut had intended for his younger son. By the time **HARTHACNUT**, 1040–1042, returned to England, he found Harold dead and himself chosen king. None the less, the kingdom he inherited was already more fragmented than it had been under his father, and his short reign was marked by the persecution of Harold's supporters rather than attempting to further his father's policies.

The weakness of **EDWARD THE CONFESSOR**, 1042–1066, contributed to his failure to unite England, prompting Norman intervention and bringing to an end the old line of Anglo-Saxon kings. Though born at Islip in Oxfordshire, Edward spent much of his childhood in Normandy. At heart he was more a French monk than an English king and had little interest in secular affairs. Edward's accession was engineered largely by Godwin, Earl of Wessex, whose daughter Edward reluctantly married. It was to balance the power of Godwin that Edward introduced Normans into Church and State offices. Though Godwin was briefly banished, he returned with popular support for his stand against Norman influence, in a position to impose terms upon Edward. After Godwin's death in the following year, his influence passed to his son Harold, whose power in the south enabled him to exploit the uncertainty over the succession; that he did this despite an oath he made to Duke William of Normandy to support his claim to the throne, gave William the moral high ground in the eyes of many in Europe, notwithstanding the fact that the oath was extracted under duress. When Edward died at his new palace in Westminster, built so that he could be close to the abbey he had founded, Edmund Ironside's grandson, Edgar the Aetheling, was nearest heir. But he was only a boy, and fear of anarchy if a minor ascended the throne made the Witan choose Harold, who may have been named by Edward on his deathbed. However, Harold's weak claim to the throne encouraged both Norway and Normandy to attempt the conquest of England.

After his hasty coronation, **HAROLD II**, 1066, spent his brief reign largely sword in hand. Harold's own brother, Tostig, in alliance with Harald Hadrada, King of Norway, landed in the north. Marching south they camped at Stamford Bridge, to the east of York, where Harold surprised them and both were slain in the defeat of their army. Four days later William landed at Pevensey in Sussex. Harold and his mounted infantry headed south, reaching London in four days. Rather than wait for the unmounted infantry from the north and a force from the south west to join him, Harold decided to give battle at once. Fought 7 miles north west of Hastings, the battle* lasted all day and was close-run; only when a feint by the Normans induced the English to abandon their

*Our information about William's relations with Harold, his invasion preparations and the actual Battle of Hastings, is derived from the Bayeux Tapestry. This strip of canvas, many yards long and half a yard wide, is embroidered with detailed scenes – the first 'strip cartoon' – and is now in the Bayeux Museum, Normandy.

shield-ring and Harold was killed by an arrow through his eye did the invaders gain the upper hand. Harold's defeat ushered in an age that would leave none in doubt that England had become an occupied country.

The Norman Conquest

It is not easy, if possible at all, to isolate and define the heritage of the Norman Conquest. For half a century before 1066 England and Normandy had been drawing closer together. Edward the Confessor himself was more Norman than English. Norman speech, habits and customs were prevalent at his court. But in the century after 1066 the followers and descendants of William the Conqueror diverted the main stream of national development and added a Latin strain to the mongrel blood of Englishmen.

Had the Conquest never happened, England would probably have become part of the northern Scandinavian world. For all its cruelty the Conquest united England to western Europe and opened the floodgates of European culture and institutions, theology, philosophy and science.

The Conquest effected a social revolution in England. The lands of the Saxon aristocracy were divided up amongst the Normans, who by c.1087 composed between 6,000 and 10,000 of a total population of about one and a half million. More important, each landowner had, in return for his land, to make an oath of allegiance to the king, and promise to provide him with mounted, armoured knights when required. The introduction of the 'feudal system', a system of land-holding in return for military obligations, provided the whole basis for medieval English society.

The Saxon machinery of government was, in large measure, retained and immensely reinforced, with a Norman monarch and the officials of his household as effective centralized controllers. Royal power was delegated in the provinces, so that government became less capricious: rebellion from Saxon or Norman was crushed with rough but equal justice. Royal justice was not only done but seen to be done. As well as giving the law a reputation for impartiality, the Normans brought with them their military arts – castle-building and fighting on horseback. They revolutionized English ecclesiastical architecture – witness Durham, Winchester, Ely and St Albans, with their rounded archways and doorways – introducing a standard plan for the great churches, and providing a point of departure for English medieval church architecture.

The Normans also transmitted large parts of the Saxon heritage – towns and villages, shires, traditions of monarchy, the basic structure of its language. They inherited a going, but run-down concern. They took over much that was indigenous and learnt from the conquered. They created a strong monarchy which, in medieval times, was gradually to complete the unification of England and obliterate the distinction between Saxons and conquering Normans, so that only Englishmen remained.

THE NORMAN KINGS
William I (The Conqueror)

Born Falaise 1027. Ascended throne 1066. Reigned 21 years.
Illegitimate son of Duke Robert the Magnificent and a tanner's daughter.
Married Matilda of Flanders.
Four sons, five daughters.
Died Rouen 1087, aged 60 years. Buried St Stephen's, Caen, Normandy.

William became Duke of Normandy at the age of seven. He married his second cousin Matilda, the daughter of the Count of Flanders, who transferred descent in the female line from the House of Wessex.

He was second cousin of Edward the Confessor. It is said that he was promised the throne by Edward (who stubbornly refused to give his wife a child, and England an heir) in 1051. In 1064, he extorted a promise along the same lines when the unfortunate Harold Godwinson, Edward's brother-in-law, was shipwrecked in Normandy.*

William's triumph over Harold (see p19) was the decisive event in the Conquest of England, but it was only a prelude to the country's subjugation. Even during his coronation at Westminster on Christmas Day 1066, a disturbance outside all but emptied the abbey. It took several years and a campaign of terror to subdue the whole country: after the south west was brought to heel, two rebellions in the north, led by earls Edwin and Morcar, were successfully defeated. The second revolt, attempted after both earls had been pardoned, provoked a savage response: between York and Durham not a house or human being visible to William's soldiers was spared. When the Domesday survey was carried out seventeen years later, many villages in the area were still without an inhabitant. The last assault on Norman hegemony came from East Anglia where Hereward, a Fenman with an aptitude for guerrilla warfare in that watery landscape, held out for some time on the Isle of Ely.

Once England was secure, William turned his attention to Scotland and Wales,

*The descent of the throne in Saxon times bore an hereditary aspect, but there was no principle of primogeniture, eg, in the tenth century only three out of eight kings immediately succeeded their fathers. The death of each king was followed by the election by the Witan (or council) of the most suitable candidate, royal birth being the prerequisite. After the Conquest the principle of primogeniture was gradually adopted.

invading the former in 1072 and compelling Malcolm III to do homage at Abernethy. Three years later he visited St David's, receiving submissions from the Welsh *en route*.

Physical evidence of the Conquest soon appeared throughout England: Saxon peasants were forced to build mounds of earth (mottes) on which fortresses of wood and later stone were erected. In London the domination of the White Tower reminded the independent Londoners of the new limitations on their freedom. From these bastions Normans enforced the confiscation of estates and their redistribution amongst those who had supported William's conquest. Feudal baronies were imposed as soon as each part of England was subjugated, resulting in some barons holding lands in different parts of the country. This had the added advantage for the monarch of preventing the consolidation of rival powers. To this end the great earldoms of late Saxon England were broken up and the shire, or county, became the principal unit of administration, superintended by sheriffs and special commissioners.

Even the French-speaking barons resented the restrictions imposed on their power by William's system of government, and as early as 1075 took up arms against him: the Norman Earl of Hereford joined Ralph the Breton, Earl of East Anglia, and the Englishman Waltheof. Their rebellion was easily contained, but it was only the first of many. Even William's eldest son, Robert, challenged his father in Normandy in 1079, and William was at war with France in 1087 when his horse stumbled in Mantes, giving him a fatal injury.

By his oath to observe the old Saxon laws and his imposition of Continental feudal customs, William effectively prevented the monarchy from exercising unlimited power, laying the ground for the development of English laws and liberties. The Church, too, stood between the king and the barons, helping to uphold a balance of power that did not infringe its own interests. Lanfranc, William's new Italian Archbishop, reorganized the English Church, and separate Church courts were established to deal with offences under canon law, an action which was to cause much trouble for the Plantagenet kings.

William the Conqueror, 'that stark man' as his subjects called him, was ruthless and cruel: although only one person was executed in his reign, thousands were mutilated, especially for breaches of the game laws – the 'New' Forest was created by him as a game park. 'He loved the tall, red deer, as if he were their father.' This penchant, however, was to sow the seed of trouble for centuries: in the eleventh century the Crown owned sixty-nine forests, almost a third of the whole acreage of the kingdom. Depriving those who lived in or near the forests of any rights in them caused great resentment, and the severe punishments for infringing forest law, enforced by Forest Courts, fed through into the draconian Game Laws of later centuries.

The *Anglo-Saxon Chronicle* gives a good impression of William's reign: 'He was mild to the good men that loved God, and beyond measure severe to the men that gainsaid his will . . . It is not to be forgotten that good peace he made in this land so that a man might go over his kingdom with his bosom full of gold . . . and no man durst slay another.'

William died at the Convent of St Gervais, near Rouen, on 9 September 1087.

The Domesday Book

The Domesday survey, 1086, was the most comprehensive and detailed record of a country's physical resources produced in Europe during the Middle Ages. William conceived the idea while at Gloucester for Christmas in 1085, though it was not referred to as 'Domesday' until the twelfth century, intended to signify that, like the Day of Judgement, there was no appeal. Its primary purpose was to maximize tax revenues; its secondary use was to provide the necessary information for the efficient administration of the feudal system. The task of gathering the data fell to Commissioners using the shire courts and interviewing sworn juries, each made up of the priest, the reeve (the lord's manager) and six villeins. The survey covered the entire country except for Durham, Northumberland, Westmorland, Cumberland, northern Lancashire, London, Winchester and a few other towns. Its scope was exhaustive: as the Saxon chronicler recorded, 'so narrowly did he cause the survey to be made that there was not one single hide nor rood of land, nor – it is shameful to tell but he thought it no shame to do – was there an ox, cow or swine that was not set down in the writ.' The two volumes are kept in the Public Record Office at Kew, London.

William II ('Rufus')

Born c.1056–1060. Ascended throne 1087. Reigned 13 years.
Third son of the Conqueror.
Never married.
Died New Forest 1100 (? accidentally shot in the eye ? murdered). Buried in Winchester Cathedral.

The Conqueror left Normandy to his eldest son, Robert, and England to his third son, William, his favourite. This arrangement was a great disappointment to Robert, a pleasure-loving knight with little control over his sparring barons. It was also a decision fraught with danger: enmity between the brothers was likely to lead to hostilities, and the division of his dominion split the loyalty of the leading Norman families, most of whom owned land on both sides of the Channel.

'Rufus', so-called because of his flaming red hair, was stern and avaricious, encouraging many Norman barons to take Robert's side. They preferred the idea of Normandy's anarchy under the easy-going Robert who made no attempt to restrict their freedoms in the way that William did in England. His admiration for a coarse chivalry and feats of arms attracted military adventurers from all over Europe, swelling his retinue with knights whose unbridled behaviour must have alienated further the Norman barons.

Rebellion came within a year of the coronation. Simultaneous uprisings by disaffected Norman barons might have been expected to triumph when William had little dependable Norman support; instead he appealed to the English, promising fair laws and taxes, and the restoration of the forests for hunting. They rallied to his call and defeated the rebels on land and Robert's invading force by sea. William kept none of his promises, and the death of Lanfranc took away the only man who attempted to mould William's moral conscience. The king's profligacy probably attracted him to the unctuous Ranulf, whose abilities at raising money were formidable. The see of Canterbury was left vacant after Lanfranc's death, and the revenues channelled into royal coffers. The practice was applied to other sees when their bishops died. Lay estates were also subject to Ranulf's skills at extracting money.

Repeated efforts by rebellious barons to overthrow William were thwarted by guile, false promises and military skill. Savage fines, mutilation or death were meted out to the plotters. William twice invaded Normandy, in 1090 and 1094. On the first occasion, after an initial defeat in the streets of Rouen, William returned in such force that Robert had no choice but to come to terms. The second was inconclusive and extremely costly. William completed the make-up of England by taking western Cumberland and Westmorland from Scotland in 1092 and building Carlisle Castle to defend his gains.

William briefly repented of his stand against the Church when illness brought him near death in 1093, prompting the appointment of an unwilling Anselm as Archbishop of Canterbury. On his recovery, conflict with Anselm was inevitable: when it came William tried to dismiss Anselm but he was deftly humiliated by a papal legate and had to be content with driving his troublesome archbishop into exile.

When Robert decided to go on a crusade, he entrusted Normandy to William by mortgaging it to him to help raise the money required for a rash but ultimately successful undertaking. William tried repeatedly to reconquer Maine, which Robert had lost, and intended to hold on to Normandy when Robert returned from the crusade. William never had the opportunity: on 1 August 1100 he was killed by an arrow while hunting in the New Forest; the site of his death is marked by the 'Rufus Stone'. The alacrity and precision with which Henry went through the motions to become king, the rewards he gave to the relatives of the suspected author of the arrow, even the fact that William's body was abandoned by the party and arrived in Winchester on a charcoal-burner's cart, make it hard to believe William's death was an accident.

Henry I

Born Selby (by tradition) 1068. Ascended throne 1100. Reigned 35 years.
Fourth son of William the Conqueror.
Married (i) Matilda of Scotland (ii) Adela of Louvain.
One daughter, one son.
Died near Rouen, 1135. Buried in Reading Abbey.

The youngest and only English-born son of William the Conqueror, Henry had suffered at the hands of both his brothers by the time he took the throne of England (see above). Though the ablest of the three, he was capable of cruelty and deceit, and his avariciousness exceeded even that of William II. None the less he was a capable and efficient ruler, who like Rufus realized the value of English support against the barons and against his elder brother. To help secure their allegiance he wisely renounced the oppressive policies of his dead brother, issuing a charter of liberties that promised to restore the laws of his father and King Edward the Elder. Anselm was recalled and Ranulf imprisoned. And he astutely married Matilda, the daughter of Malcolm, king of Scotland, which made for peace with Scotland and pleased the English, Matilda being great grand-daughter of Edmund Ironside. Henry's promises proved as worthless as those of William II, the exigencies of his costly wars and growing bureaucracy taking precedence over the restoration of rights. Though the death penalty for crimes against property was restored and sentences were often savagely harsh, they were not arbitrary as they had been under William Rufus. All was done within the law.

The prospect of war with Normandy after Robert's return from the crusade was precipitated by the escape from prison of Ranulf, who persuaded Robert that the barons would support him if he invaded England. Robert landed at Portsmouth, and at Alton in Hampshire the Norman army met the local fyrd. Henry was able to prevent combat by a few promises, which he was not to keep, but Robert of Bellême, the most powerful baron in England, continued with his brothers to oppose the king and had to be defeated.

In exile in Normandy, Robert of Bellême formed the nucleus of a growing band of dispossessed and discontented barons whom Duke Robert was powerless to control, even if he had the inclination to do so. Henry used his brother's weakness as a pretext to invade Normandy in 1105, in order to destroy the external threat posed by the barons. After a slow start and unsuccessful negotiations to avoid combat, Henry routed the Norman forces at Tinchebrai, thereby uniting England and Normandy. Henry's brother spent the rest of his life imprisoned, first at Devizes and later at Cardiff. Surprisingly Henry did not imprison or constrain his nephew William the Clito whom many Normans regarded as Robert's rightful successor; for the rest of Henry's reign William provided the cause for further fighting between Normandy and rebellious barons in alliance with Louis VI, king of France. When Louis appealed to the Pope on behalf of William the Clito's claim, Henry's brilliant use of dynastic marriages paid off: the Pope was keen to make peace with the Holy Roman Emperor to whom Henry's daughter Matilda was married, so he was naturally reluctant to offend his father-in-law. William the Atheling, Henry's only legitimate son and heir to the English throne, was accepted as heir to Normandy too.

The conflict between king and Church continued under Henry, principally over the right to appoint bishops, which both claimed. The Pope had granted William I the right to invest his own bishops, but had no wish to extend the concession to his sons. After years of negotiations in a politer refrain than that between Anselm and William II, a compromise was reached that still left Henry with substantial influence and income from sees.

A major contribution to England's institutions was Henry's reorganization of the judicial system and the methods of raising taxes. He greatly extended the scope of the Curia Regis (King's Court), in future acting as an advisory body and as a court of law, as well as supervising taxation. Members of this court were sent out to bring even the remote districts into contact with royal taxation, as well as to make people familiar with royal justice. The extension of the Curia Regis's powers paved the way for its evolution into a Parliament, its inner members forming the Privy Council and the King's Bench. Henry's greatest agent was Roger, Bishop of Salisbury, who it is said commended himself to the king by the speed with which he could get through church services. Roger was once a poor Norman priest and an example of the way Henry appointed humble men of ability.

In 1120 Henry's legitimate son was drowned in the tragedy of the White Ship. It was expected that Henry would nominate his favourite nephew, Stephen of Blois, but instead, to English dismay, he chose as his successor his daughter Matilda who married as her second husband Geoffrey, Count of Anjou – Geoffrey Plantagenet. (Though Henry remarried, no children were born.) But when Henry died in 1135 of a surfeit of lampreys, the Council, considering a woman unfit to rule, offered the throne to Stephen.

Stephen

Born c.1097. Ascended throne 1135. Reigned 19 years.
Married Matilda of Boulogne.
One son, two daughters.
Died Dover 1154. Buried in Faversham Abbey.

For seventy years after the Conquest, England had the benefits of strong government and the beginnings of rational justice. During the 'nineteen long winters' of Stephen's reign, England again knew what it was like to be governed by a weak king. Known as the anarchy, Stephen's years on the throne have been described as 'not a reign but a war of succession'.

There was a number of claimants to the throne, but the help of Stephen's brother Henry, Bishop of Winchester, in securing the support of the Church for Stephen's coronation was crucial. The barons' dislike of Henry's daughter Matilda, combined with Stephen's personal charm and wealth, gave him an advantage that he was soon to squander. His lack of resolve became manifest when David I, king of Scotland, invaded; in command of an army large enough to impose terms, Stephen weakly conceded Cumberland and Westmorland. His neglect to secure Normandy by thoroughly suppressing mutinous barons proved fatal to the peace in England: left in Normandy when Stephen returned to England, Henry's powerful illegitimate son, Earl Robert, renounced his allegiance to Stephen and transferred it to Matilda, prompting many in England to do the same. Stephen's ineptitude alienated other supporters, including Bishop Roger of Salisbury and others in the Church, just as Matilda and Earl Robert landed in Sussex in 1139, Robert making for the principal rebel castle, at Bristol, while Matilda installed herself at Arundel.

The nobility, during the decade of civil war that followed, threw in their lot with both sides, often to the highest bidder, and built castles from which they terrorized their areas. The countryside was ravaged, crops were destroyed, cattle were driven off and people starved. It was, as the chronicler put it, a time when 'Christ and his saints slept'.

At a critical battle outside Lincoln in 1141, Stephen was captured and taken to Bristol where he was imprisoned in chains. Only his queen and William of Ypres in command of Flemish mercenaries held out in Essex and parts of Kent. Matilda was on the point of being crowned when her arrogant rescission of grants made by Stephen alienated many barons. Her imposition of heavy taxes on Londoners induced them to take up arms, compelling Matilda to flee to Oxford. At another pivotal battle, at Winchester, Stephen's queen restored the balance by capturing Earl Robert. An exchange of Stephen and Earl Robert was arranged. The war dragged on in stalemate until in 1147, with the death of Earl Robert, Matilda gave up and left. But still the war dragged on, some in support of her son Henry Plantagenet, rather than Matilda. Stephen lost the Church's support over his demands that his son Eustace should be crowned, and his loyal queen died. When Eustace, too, died Stephen lost heart; the Treaty of Winchester ended the wretched war, confirming Henry Plantagenet as heir to the throne. Henry had only a year to wait for it.

THE PLANTAGENET KINGS

Henry II was the first of a long line of fourteen Plantagenet kings. Their reigns stretched over more than three hundred years of English history, from the accession of Henry II in 1154 to the death of Richard III on Bosworth Field in 1485.

The name 'Plantagenet' was originally a nickname given to Count Geoffrey of Anjou, father of Henry II, because of the gay yellow broom flower (*Planta genista*) which he wore in his helmet. In time this emblem was embodied in the family arms.

For the sake of convenience the Plantagenets are usually divided up under the names of the three related families of Anjou, Lancaster and York, from amongst whose members the fourteen monarchs came. The next section presents the outline story of the Angevins, the Lancastrians and the Yorkists.

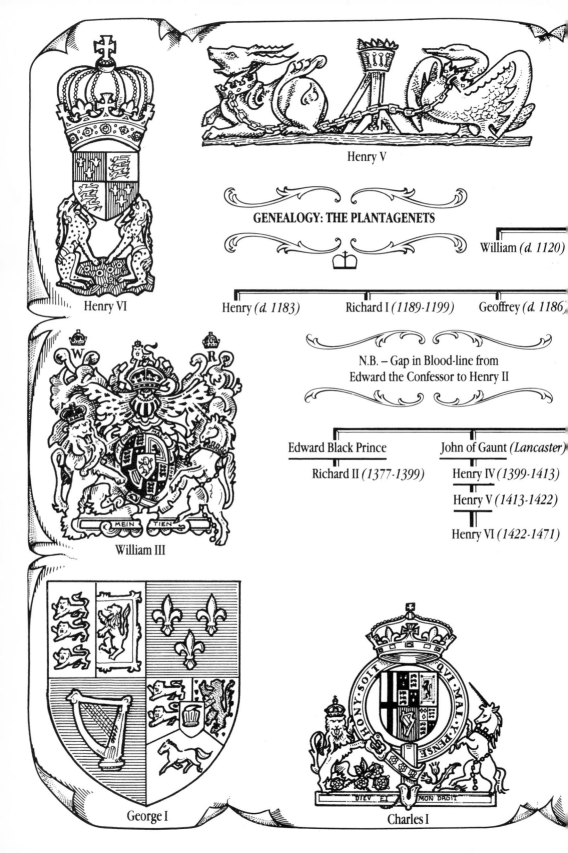

Henry V

GENEALOGY: THE PLANTAGENETS

William *(d. 1120)*

Henry *(d. 1183)*   Richard I *(1189-1199)*   Geoffrey *(d. 1186)*

N.B. – Gap in Blood-line from
Edward the Confessor to Henry II

Edward Black Prince   John of Gaunt *(Lancaster)*

Richard II *(1377-1399)*   Henry IV *(1399-1413)*

Henry V *(1413-1422)*

Henry VI *(1422-1471)*

Henry VI

William III

George I

Charles I

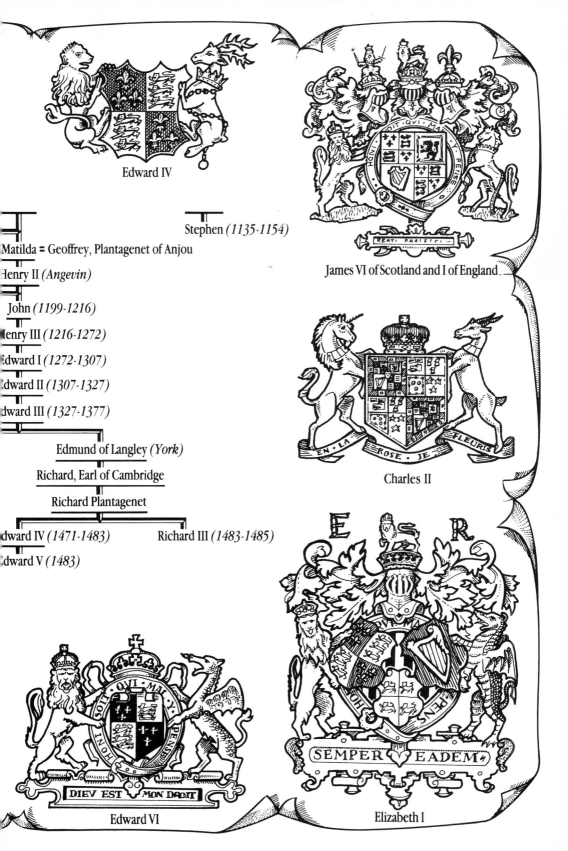

Edward IV

James VI of Scotland and I of England

Charles II

Stephen *(1135-1154)*

Matilda **=** Geoffrey, Plantagenet of Anjou

Henry II *(Angevin)*

John *(1199-1216)*

Henry III *(1216-1272)*

Edward I *(1272-1307)*

Edward II *(1307-1327)*

Edward III *(1327-1377)*

Edmund of Langley *(York)*

Richard, Earl of Cambridge

Richard Plantagenet

Edward IV *(1471-1483)*   Richard III *(1483-1485)*

Edward V *(1483)*

Edward VI

Elizabeth I

Henry II

Born Le Mans 1133. Ascended throne 1154. Reigned 35 years.
Eldest son of Matilda.
Married Eleanor of Aquitaine.
Five sons, three daughters.
Died Chinon 1189, aged 56. Buried at Fontevrault.
First of the Angevin kings.

Henry II was a European ruler rather than an English king. His empire stretched from the Solway almost to the Mediterranean, and from the Somme to the Pyrenees. The size of Henry's inheritance was the result of two key marriages: his father's to Matilda who, as daughter of Henry I, was the probable heiress to England and Normandy; and his own to the vivacious Eleanor of Aquitaine. By the time he was crowned king at the age of twenty-one, Henry's wealth exceeded that of any other prince in Europe, even his nominal overlord, the king of France. To his inheritance he added Ireland, a mission entrusted to him by Pope Adrian IV (Nicholas Brakespear, the only Englishman ever to be Pope [1154–9]). And through diplomacy he forced Malcolm IV, the young king of Scotland, to return the counties of Westmorland, Cumberland and Northumberland which Stephen had lost.

The general aim of his policy in England was to undo all the harm caused by Stephen's reign. He triumphed brilliantly over the nobility, but he was, in turn, worsted by the Church.

His first concern was to restore order. Castles built by the rebellious nobles were demolished, royal castles were resumed, along with Crown lands. Henry was then able to plan for the future. He raised new taxes (scutage, or shield money) from the landholders in lieu of their feudal military obligations. The old feudal limit of forty days' military service was of little use to a monarch who might need to take troops to Gascony. By a command of 1181 the basis of an English militia force was laid. Henry now had two armies: the mercenary army, paid for by the new taxes, and the militia; whilst his powerful subjects and their followers got less practice in the arts of war. As a result their attention turned to the lands they held and the techniques of agriculture, which were developed most skilfully by Cistercian monks on their estates. The stone castle gave way to the stone manor house, and the tournament became the only means for some to display their martial skills (Henry's son Geoffrey was killed at a tournament in Paris).

Royal justice was revived. Judges from the King's courts were again sent into the shires, where they now combined with twelve local men to administer the law; in this way Henry laid the foundations of Common Law (a law applicable to the whole country, free of local customs), emanating from the Curia Regis, and of the modern English jury system. Gradually trial by judges, with the assistance of jurymen, replaced the barbarous trials by ordeal and trials by battle, in both criminal and civil cases. (For a trial by ordeal the accused was made to plunge his head into boiling water or carry a piece of red-hot metal. His guilt or innocence was decided by the speed with which the wounds healed.) The jury was not yet a group of 'outside' people brought in to hear and decide on a case, but witnesses to the fact.

These reforms were not inspired by Henry's high-mindedness but because the courts were his chosen instrument for enforcing and extorting payment of revenues. By the end of Henry's reign, the English had for the first time become accustomed to paying their taxes, to co-operating in government and to expecting fair play in the law courts. His system was so fundamentally efficient that it continued to work even under the weak rulers that followed him.

But, unjustly, it is probably for his quarrel with Thomas Becket that Henry is chiefly remembered. The Church of England was claiming more independence from lay control than Henry was prepared to allow. He wished to retain the right to nominate his own appointees to vacant bishoprics and to try in his own courts clerks* who had committed a crime, for the Church courts (introduced by William I) had no power of life and death – a cleric could only be downgraded. Any wrongdoer who could read a Latin text from the Bible passed the test of clerical status (the so-called 'neck verse'), and could claim 'benefit of clergy', or immunity from the king's justice. In the same way a criminal fleeing from justice could claim 'sanctuary' in the precincts of a church. The Constitutions of Clarendon ended the clergy's immunity from State prosecution by instigating a system whereby a clerk accused of a felony would appear first in a lay court, then be tried by a Church court and, if found guilty, be brought back to the lay court for sentence.

Becket, Henry's Chancellor and one-time convivial friend, turned ascetic and quarrelled bitterly with Henry over these questions, even rejecting the Constitutions of Clarendon. He was exiled from 1164 to 1170. In his stand against the king, Becket was not even supported by all the bishops, and lay opinion inclined to the king. Only Becket's murder gave him posthumous victory, thereby allowing anyone who could make a stab at reading to commit serious crimes without fear of heavy penalties. This only served to attract some dubious characters to holy orders in order to obtain protection from State law. But Henry stood firm over advowsons, and prevented them becoming the prerogative of the Roman Court, though this remained for centuries a cause for struggle between Pope and the patrons of English livings.

*A 'clerk' in the Middle Ages was anyone in orders, from the Archbishop of Canterbury to the humblest verger – about one in fifty of the population.

When Becket returned from exile he proceeded to anger Henry still further. The murder of Becket at Canterbury Cathedral on 29 December 1170, by men believing they were acting on Henry's orders, gave the Church a martyr and ultimately a saint, whilst Henry lost all. Not until the Reformation did royal power prevail over the Church. Chaucer's epic work reflected the popularity of the cult of St Thomas, giving to the language the word 'canter' as the pace at which pilgrims should ride.

The closing years of the reign were troublesome. Henry subjects on both sides of the Channel rebelled, and it was only with the aid of mercenaries and the militia that the realm was quietened at home and abroad. Much of the trouble was caused by the frustrations of Henry's sons, incited to rebellion by their mother, who were supported by the kings of France and Scotland. It was while Henry was fighting Philip of France in 1188 that his son Richard joined the French king. Military reverses compelled Henry to grant a peace treaty which granted a pardon to Richard's followers. Shortly before he died, Henry was devastated to find on the list the name of his favourite son John.

Richard I (Coeur-de-Lion)

Born Oxford 1157. Ascended throne 1189. Reigned 10 years.
Third son of Henry II.
Married Berengaria of Navarre.
No issue.
Died Châlus-Chabrol 1199, aged 42. Buried at Fontevrault; his heart at Rouen.

Richard I had little English blood in him. He spent only ten months of his ten years' reign in England, and there is some doubt as to whether he could speak English (French remained the language of the upper classes until Edward III's time). He regarded his kingdom solely as a source of revenue for his crusading ventures: 'I would have sold London itself if I could have found a rich enough buyer,' he is reputed to have said. Many towns benefited by the Charters which they gained from Richard in return for financial assistance.

Henry II had promised to undertake a crusade against the Moslems to expiate the murder of Becket, a promise not altogether disinterested, as the Angevins acquired a title by marriage to the kingdom of Jerusalem. He bequeathed this promise to his successor and, though obedience to his father's wishes had not so far been his strong point, Richard took part in the best known of all the crusades, the third.

Its aim was to free the Holy Land from the Turks, who were Moslems. It failed to achieve this, but Jerusalem was made easier of access for Christian pilgrims. With Philip I, Richard left for Palestine in 1190, wintering in Sicily where Richard's sister Joanna lived as queen to King William. A second delay in reaching the coast of Outremer was caused by the insolent treatment of Richard's men by Isaac Commenus, ruler of Cyprus and pretender to the Byzantine throne. Richard was so enraged by Commenus's behaviour that, after marrying Berengaria of Navarre on the island, he conquered it before leaving to join the siege of Acre. The city fell in July 1191, after which the victors fell out amongst themselves, several deciding to return home, leaving Richard unquestioned leader of the crusade. There followed an example of his ruthlessness when, unjustly suspecting Saladin of breaking the terms of Acre's surrender, he slaughtered 2,500 men with their wives and children in full view of their fellow countrymen. But for his exploits in winning a total victory over Saladin's army at Arsuf and for taking Jaffa and other towns, Richard earned the admiration of all Christendom.

On his way home Richard was captured by the Duke of Austria, who sold him to the Emperor Henry VI. So a crusade begun for the rescue of the Holy Land ended with the sale of one Christian monarch to another. For fourteen months, until his ransom was paid, Richard was imprisoned in a secret imperial castle, where, legend tells us, he was found at last by his minstrel, Blondel. Never again did an English king leave his realm to go crusading.

Richard's absentee rule ushered in a period of some eighty years during which the Crown was weaker than in the previous century or so. The government of the country was fortunately in the hands of capable deputies, who successfully combated the ambitions of the king's brother, John, and the intrigues of the nobles, in addition to raising enormous sums of money for the expenses of the crusade and the King's ransom. The situation in Normandy, however, was such that Richard had to spend the last five years of his life fighting Philip, to whom his brother John had sworn homage in return for Richard's lands. It was while besieging a castle that he was killed.

John

Born Oxford 1167. Ascended throne 1199. Reigned 17 years.
Fourth son of Henry II.
Married (i) Isabel of Gloucester (ii) Isabella of Angoulême.
Two sons, three daughters by second wife.
Died Newark 1216, aged (?)49. Buried at Worcester.

The archetype of the 'wicked king', John was the fourth son of Henry II, the child of his father's middle age. Not without some administrative ability, especially as regards the collection of money, he was yet cruel and avaricious.

He was nicknamed 'Lackland', because his brothers were given territory by their father when he received none until made King of Ireland in 1177. However, his campaign there in 1185-6 was disastrous and his brother recalled him for misconduct.

Though John had intrigued against Richard while his brother was on crusade, they were reconciled, and on his death-bed Richard made John his heir.

John continued to live up to his nickname, for in 1204 he lost Normandy and Anjou to the King of France, and by 1205 only a fragment remained of the vast Angevin empire. In the long run this enforced insularity fostered the growth of the English nation state.

In 1205 John quarrelled with the Church, because he refused to accept Stephen Langton, the Pope's nominee, as Archbishop of Canterbury. In 1207 England was laid under an interdict, and John was excommunicated two years later. The dispute ended with John's abject surrender to Innocent 111, one of the greatest of medieval popes.

The loss of England's French possessions, the ignominious failure of his quarrel with Rome, allied to misgovernment and the raising of extortionate taxes, united against John the articulate elements of society. John's conduct encouraged men of intellect to conceive of law as having an existence independent of and above the king. The gradual removal of feudal balances and responsibilities, begun by Henry II, required the substitution of other mechanisms to prevent despotism. It was John's extortions to finance incompetent expeditions to recover his Angevin inheritance that proved the final straw: during his absence on the Continent fighting against the French king, a project crowned with failure at the Battle of Bouvines in 1214, a party led by Langton came into existence. This is the first time in English history that a consensus of influential opinion enabled concerted action to be taken on such a scale against bad government. Londoners and the clergy supported the initiative of the Archbishop and the barons.

A demand was made for the confirmation of popular liberties. After the barons' forces had assembled at Stamford and marched to London, the king capitulated and on Monday 15 June 1215, on the small island of Runnymede in the Thames near Windsor, sealed the Magna Carta, the Great Charter, which restated the rights of the Church, the barons and all in the land. The three most important clauses laid down

1 That the Church was free to choose its own officials.
2 That no money, over and above certain payments, was to be paid by the king's feudal tenants without their previous consent.
3 That no freeman* was to be punished except according to the laws of the land.

Langton's key role was all the more remarkable for being contrary to the Pope's wishes; since John's agreement to hold England as a fief of the Papacy, Innocent III had supported him in the conflict. John soon reneged on his agreement with Langton and the barons, but after the barons invited the French Dauphin to lead them, the situation was reversed. John died at Newark, after eating peaches and beer, in the midst of an invasion, bequeathing enormous problems to his nine-year-old son.

*Medieval society distinguished, of course, between servile and free men.

Henry III

Born Winchester 1207. Ascended throne 1216. Reigned 56 years.
Married Eleanor of Provence.
Four sons, two daughters.
Died Westminster 1272, aged 65. Buried at Westminster.

Henry III was born, and spent almost his entire life, in England. He was only nine years old when he came to the throne, but the government of the country was in the hands of capable deputies until he declared himself of age in 1227. During this period the French invaders were expelled and the few remaining adherents of John's party were crushed. Five years later Henry deprived the former Regent Hubert de Burgh of all his offices, and in 1234 took the administration into his own hands.

There followed a period of poor government, for in spite of some redeeming features Henry was a weak, untrustworthy character. He combated his poverty, a legacy from his father and uncle, by ruthless, extortionate taxation, yet engaged in costly, fruitless wars. He mounted three equally disastrous campaigns to France, which would have cost what Continental possessions remained from John's losses had it not been for the generosity of Louis IX. Moreover, Henry's spineless reluctance to oppose any decree from the Pope meant unsuitable appointments to benefices, the most flagrant example being the Pope's promise of rewarding the loyalty of Romans with the next 300 benefices that fell vacant in England. Without a bulwark to resist such arbitrary actions, anti-papal sentiments flourished, anticipating the growing resentment that would fuel the Reformation. But Henry's crowning folly was his agreement to finance papal wars in Sicily in return for the Sicilian crown for his son Edmund. The exorbitant sums Henry demanded, combined with the absence of any benefit for England, roused the barons to fury, leading to a period of civil war out of which would emerge an important development in the steps towards a Parliament.

Led by Henry's brother-in-law, Simon de Montfort, the barons compelled Henry to abide by the Provisions of Oxford, curtailing his power. When Henry repudiated them and Louis IX, to whom the matter had been referred, annulled them, de Montfort and the reformists fought and defeated the king at Lewes. But Henry's opponents were divided into two distinct interest groups: on the one hand the conservative barons and on the other the reforming barons and lesser gentry supported by many of the clergy, the students of Oxford University and the citizens of London. This split was cleverly exploited by Prince Edward, leading key barons to desert de Montfort and enabling the king to defeat him at the Battle of Evesham in 1265. De Montfort died on the battlefield, but his cause was not lost on Prince Edward who realized the need for the king to rule under the law and equally importantly that the Crown could be stronger for working through Parliament rather than in opposition to the nation. He appreciated the value of the consultative process set up by de Montfort when representatives from the shires and boroughs came to Parliament to discuss State and judicial affairs.

If he was a failure as a king, Henry III was probably the greatest of all patrons of medieval ecclesiastical architecture. During his reign the plain, massive style of the Normans gave way to the pointed arches, lancet windows, flying buttresses and elaborate decorations which are characteristic of the Early English and Gothic styles. The majority of English cathedrals had some portion of their fabric remodelled: Westminster Abbey was rebuilt; Salisbury Cathedral was built between 1220 and 1266.

During this long reign Franciscan and Dominican friars* set up establishments in England. This gave an impetus to works of charity and also to university teaching at Oxford and Cambridge.

By the time Henry died in 1272, he had all but relinquished government to his son.

Edward I ('Longshanks')

Born Westminster 1239. Ascended throne 1272. Reigned 35 years.
Married (i) Eleanor of Castille (ii) Margaret of France.
Three sons, five daughters by first wife; two sons, one daughter by second wife.
Died Burgh by Sands 1307, aged 68. Buried at Westminster.

Edward I was an authoritarian statesman, a lawyer and a soldier. In these different capacities he modernized many aspects of English life. When he died at the beginning of the fourteenth century, much in English government, society and law had taken on a permanent form that in essentials was to survive the Hundred Years War and the Wars of the Roses.

Paradoxically, given his autocratic temperament, Edward has been called the father to the 'Mother of all Parliaments'. To his 'Model Parliament' in 1295 he summoned representatives from amongst the nobility, the greater and lesser clergy, the knights of the shires, the burgesses of the cities – thereby bringing Lords and Commons together for the first time. The growing demands on the government for justice and general administration meant that by now the feudal revenues were inadequate; Edward needed money from the new merchant class, and to summon national Parliaments was the only way to get it. In this way parliament became the established method of conducting public business. The need for finance was also behind the conflict with both the Church and the barons over taxation. Even a revival of anti-Semitism was used as an excuse to

---

*'Friar' Tuck, companion of Robin Hood, in John's reign is an anachronism.

expel the Jews in 1290 so that the Crown would benefit financially from forteitures.

Edward completed the judicial reforms begun by Henry II. The courts of King's Bench, Common Pleas and Exchequer were given separate staffs of judges and officials; and a Court of Equity, the Chancery Court, was set up to give redress where the other courts could provide no remedy. A whole series of Acts dealt with the position of the Church, the enforcement of public order, trade and the position of great landholders. 'Conservators of the Peace' were created, forerunners of the Justices of the Peace created by Edward III.

As usual the drain on royal finances was caused largely by costly wars. Edward possessed the necessary martial skills, learnt during the conflicts of his father's reign and on crusade in Egypt and Syria in 1270–4. For five years Edward had to fight Philip the Fair after the French king had invaded Gascony. Edward's ambition to rule over an undivided nation was checked by the independence of Wales and Scotland. The sustained opposition of Llywelyn ap Gruffudd from 1277 to his death in 1282 made the conquest of Wales a lengthy campaign, but English administration and law was extended to the Principality through the Statute of Rhuddlan (1284). Edward began the construction of fourteen new castles to secure his gains. The king's eldest son was created Prince of Wales in 1301, a title since borne by all male heirs to the throne.

Right until the day of his death Edward waged war unsuccessfully against the Scots, led first by Sir William Wallace and later by Robert Bruce. But the epitaph on his tomb at Westminster bears witness to the magnificence of his failure in Scotland: 'Here lies Edward the Hammer of the Scots'.

Edward II

Born Caernarfon 1284. Ascended throne 1307. Reigned 20 years (deposed).
Son of Edward I.
Married Isabella of France.
Two sons, two daughters.
Died Berkeley Castle 1327 (murdered), aged 43. Buried in Gloucester Cathedral.

Edward II was Edward I's greatest failure. Feeble and perverted, he did nothing to carry on his father's work of consolidation. Yet by default, his laziness and incompetence strengthened the influence of Parliament, and the bureaucracy was improved by various reforms.

Addicted to worthless favourites, first Piers Gaveston, and later the Despensers (father and son), the king aroused the wrath of the nobles by leaving Gaveston as guardian of the kingdom when he left for France in 1308 to marry Isabella, daughter of

Philip IV. Besides Gaveston's status as a 'foreigner' (from Gascony) and the nature of his relationship with Edward, the barons were incensed by his habit of giving them nicknames. The barons forced Edward to banish Gaveston to Ireland in 1309, and his return led to the imposition of further limitations on royal power through the Ordinances of 1311, which again banished the king's favourite. Edward's attempts to circumvent the Ordinances and his recall of Gaveston led to armed revolt in which Gaveston was captured and beheaded.

The next fiasco was Edward's efforts to impose his rule on Scotland: despite invading with a large army, Edward was soundly defeated by Robert Bruce at the Battle of Bannockburn in 1314. This and Bruce's capture of Berwick four years later settled the question of Scottish independence until the Union of England and Scotland in 1707. Edward's standing was so low that he was forced to relinquish authority to his cousin Thomas, Earl of Lancaster, who had led opposition to the king – the first indication of the struggle that was to develop between the Angevins and the younger Lancastrian branch of the family. Earl Thomas's ineptitude allowed Edward, with the help of his new favourite Hugh le Despenser, to reassert his will by force, execute Thomas and annul the Ordinances.

Queen Isabella now headed the opposition to the husband she despised, taking Prince Edward with her to France, where she fell in love with a disaffected noble, Roger de Mortimer, Baron of Wigmore. Together they invaded England, landing in Suffolk. The Despensers were executed, and Edward, after being captured in South Wales, forced to abdicate. A rescue attempt on Berkeley Castle, where he was imprisoned, prompted his murder in September 1327.

The Hundred Years War, 1337–1453

The struggle between England and France was carried on intermittently during the reigns of five English kings. The causes of the conflict included grievances over English territory and sovereignty in France, English commercial activity in Flanders, French support for Scottish independence, and the claim of Edward III, through his mother, Isabella, daughter of Philip IV, to the French crown.

Inevitably for a war carried on over a century, the fortunes of the two combatants fluctuated: until 1360 the advantage lay with England. The great naval victory of Sluys (1340) when the French fleet was surprised in the harbour, was followed by the famous English victories at Crécy (1346) and Poitiers (1356). At Crécy, the important role of the English bowmen and the exploits of the Black Prince in securing victory have become legendary. The English army at Poitiers was led by the Black Prince and won a decisive victory in which the French king was captured; King John was unable to raise the ransom demanded and died in London in 1364, The Treaty of Brétigny gave to England extensive land in return for giving up all claim to the French throne.

With the accession of the Black Prince in 1376, and the accession of Richard II (1377–99), English fortunes reached their lowest ebb with the defeat of the English fleet at La Rochelle (1372), though a Franco-Castilian invasion was thwarted off Margate in 1387. The reign of Henry IV (1399–1413) began a period of improvement, which was continued by Henry V (1413–22) at Harfleur and Agincourt (both 1415), marked by the Treaty of Troyes (1420) which allowed for the marriage of Henry to Catherine of Valois and made him heir to the French throne.

Henry's premature death did not end the run of English successes; it was only when Charles VII and Joan of Arc defeated the forces besieging Orléans (1429) that the tide turned. By 1453 Calais was all that remained of English possessions in France.

Edward III

Born Windsor Castle 1312. Ascended throne 1327. Reigned 50 years.
Son of Edward II.
Married Philippa of Hainault (the groom was aged 16, the bride 14).
Six sons, five daughters.
Died Sheen Palace 1377, aged 65. Buried at Westminster.

Edward was hastily crowned king when his father was deposed by his mother and Roger de Mortimer. His marriage to Philippa of Hainault in 1328 was arranged before his coronation, and it was a further two years before he took control of the government, ordering the arrest of Mortimer at Nottingham and the imprisonment of his mother. Mortimer was hanged at Tyburn, and his mother was banished to Castle Rising in Norfolk where she spent the last twenty-eight years of her life.

The main interest of the long reign of Edward III lies in the opening stages of the Hundred Years War with France. Ostensibly the war began, in 1337, to support Edward's claim to the French throne,* a pretence marked by Edward's quartering of the lilies of France beside the leopards of England on his coat of arms. In reality the war was, in origin, an attempt to retain control of Gascony and the wine trade centred on Bordeaux; and to keep open the connections between the English wool traders and the woollen markets of Flanders.

Sluys (1340), a naval battle, gave England control of the Channel. Though spectacular victories, neither Crécy (1346) nor Poitiers (1356) achieved much in the longer term. Calais, after a twelve months' siege (1347), passed into English hands for the next hundred years. It was in this phase of the war that the king's eldest son, Edward

---

*A claim not finally surrendered until 1802.

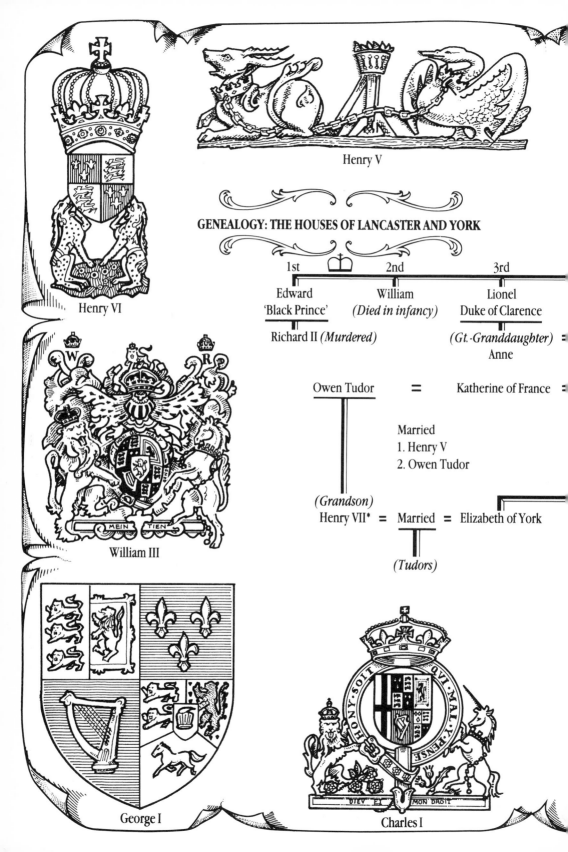

Henry V

GENEALOGY: THE HOUSES OF LANCASTER AND YORK

1st	2nd	3rd
Edward	William	Lionel
'Black Prince'	*(Died in infancy)*	Duke of Clarence
Richard II *(Murdered)*		*(Gt.-Granddaughter)* =
		Anne

Owen Tudor = Katherine of France =

Married
1. Henry V
2. Owen Tudor

(Grandson)
Henry VII* = Married = Elizabeth of York

(Tudors)

Henry VI

William III

George I

Charles I

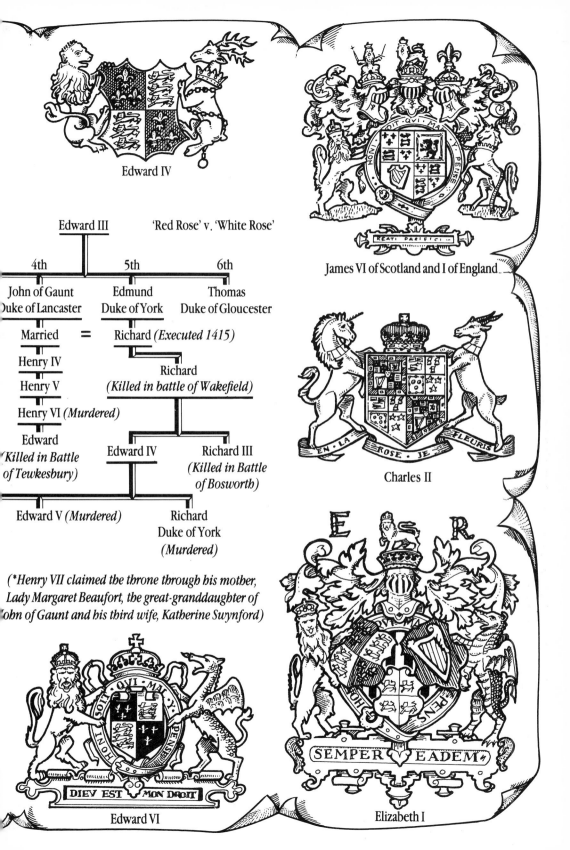

Edward IV

Edward III

'Red Rose' v. 'White Rose'

4th	5th	6th
John of Gaunt Duke of Lancaster	Edmund Duke of York	Thomas Duke of Gloucester

Married = Richard *(Executed 1415)*

Henry IV

Richard *(Killed in battle of Wakefield)*

Henry V

Henry VI *(Murdered)*

Edward *(Killed in Battle of Tewkesbury)*

Edward IV

Richard III *(Killed in Battle of Bosworth)*

Edward V *(Murdered)*

Richard Duke of York *(Murdered)*

(*Henry VII claimed the throne through his mother, Lady Margaret Beaufort, the great-granddaughter of John of Gaunt and his third wife, Katherine Swynford)

James VI of Scotland and I of England

Charles II

Edward VI

Elizabeth I

(1330–76), known to history as the 'Black Prince' (either because of the colour of his armour or, more likely, because of his foul Angevin temper), covered himself with glory.

The outbreak of bubonic plague, the 'Black Death', in 1348–50 removed a third of the population of England and undermined military strength. Originating in China and affecting the whole of Europe, the plague entered England through Melcombe Regis (now Weymouth) in 1348, and soon reached Bristol, Oxford and London. It inevitably raised the price of labour and weakened further the waning feudal system.

In 1360 the Treaty of Brétigny brought the war to a close. When Edward III died in 1377 all that was left of the English conquests were five fortified towns and the coastal lands around them.

Hostilities with Scotland were also resumed when Edward tried to bring an end to Scottish independence: supporting Edward Baliol's coronation in 1332, Edward invaded Scotland to defeat his rival, David II, at Halidon Hill near Berwick, but within five months Baliol had to flee. In 1346 David invaded England while Edward was fighting in France; Queen Philippa proved equal to the occasion by raising an army which defeated and captured David at Neville's Cross near Durham.

After Queen Philippa's death in 1369, Edward retreated to Windsor where he became increasingly senile. Public finances were in a parlous state, Edward's rapacious mistress Alice Perrers helped to erode the residual goodwill of the people and the sadness caused by the death of the Black Prince clouded his last years. He relinquished government to his fourth son, John of Gaunt, and reputedly died alone.

During Edward's long reign, many changes took place in England. Parliament, now divided into two Houses, met regularly to vote supplies for the conduct of the war. 'Treason' was defined by statute for the first time in 1352. The office of JP was created in 1361. In 1362 English replaced French as the official language of the law courts. Within twenty years John Wycliffe and the Lollards (the first 'protestants') were aiding their cause with the first 'English' translation of the Bible, and already Chaucer was writing 'English' masterpieces. The new merchant class and the spread of lay learning were building a national civilization.

Richard II

Born Bordeaux 1367. Ascended throne 1377. Reigned 22 years (deposed).
Son of the Black Prince and grandson of Edward III.
Married (i) Anne of Bohemia (ii) Isabella of France.
No issue.
Died Pontefract Castle 1400 (? murdered), aged 33. Buried (i) King's Langley
(ii) Westminster.

Richard II: artist and date unknown *(The National Portrait Gallery, London)*.

Richard II succeeded his grandfather in 1377 at the age of ten, at a time of social unrest. Though government was entrusted to a council of twelve, it was dominated by John of Gaunt, Richard's uncle, until the fourteen-year-old king displayed a remarkable ability to defuse the dangerous threat posed by the Peasants' Revolt when 100,000 men from Essex and Kent marched on London. The Black Death had been followed by rapid increases in wages and prices; Parliament had passed legislation to restrain wages, but prices were not similarly regulated, and a series of poll taxes proved the last straw.

After seizing Rochester Castle, the men of Kent under Wat Tyler joined forces with the rebels from Essex and entered the city of London, destroying John of Gaunt's manor. Richard met the Essex men and persuaded them to return home by agreeing to meet their demands. The Kent rebels, meanwhile, burned Temple Bar, occupied the Tower of London and executed the Chancellor and Archbishop of Canterbury, Simon of Sudbury, before meeting the king at Smithfield. During negotiations the Mayor of London killed Wat Tyler, but Richard rode amongst the rebels and by granting their demands induced them to disperse. The other major uprising, in East Anglia, was ruthlessly put down by the Bishop of Norwich. By September the revolt had been suppressed and Richard's promises withdrawn.

After the Peasants' Revolt, John of Gaunt receded into the background, concentrating on winning his claim through his second wife of the crown of Castile.

Richard had only himself to blame for being 'the last of the Angevins'. He proved to be extravagant, unjust and faithless. His only good act was to terminate the struggle with France in 1396. His final undoing was to make plain his wish to abandon Parliamentary government, now an established part of national life. Richard never forgave Parliament or the lords who impeached his favourites in 1388, exacting vengeance a decade later when he had murdered, beheaded or banished those who had opposed him.

Richard's reign marked the beginning of the long struggle for the Crown between the descendants of Edward III, led first by John of Gaunt, Edward's fourth son, and then by Gaunt's son, Henry Bolingbroke. When Richard deprived Henry Bolingbroke of his father's estates on his death in 1399, he provoked his downfall: Henry landed at Ravenspur in Yorkshire while Richard was in Ireland. On his return, without an army he was obliged to submit to Henry at Flint. He resigned the Crown and was deposed by Parliament, which chose Henry as his successor. From the Tower, Richard was sent to Pontefract Castle where he was probably murdered to put a stop to risings in his favour. The conflicting claims that would lead to the Wars of the Roses had taken their first victim.

The Wars of the Roses

The Wars of the Roses were a series of struggles for the Crown which lasted over a century and affected the reigns of seven English kings, from Richard II to Henry VII, though armed conflict formed a part only between 1455 and 1485. The name derived from the red and white roses of the houses of Lancaster and York, respectively.

The trouble started with Edward III's eleven children. He died leaving four surviving sons and some daughters, so that the succession could be disputed amongst too many. In addition, the marriages of royal children with the sons and daughters of powerful noble families created families which were semi-royal.

In 1399 Henry IV of Lancaster usurped the throne from the last Angevin king, Richard II. In 1461 the Yorkists in turn usurped the throne, when Edward IV deposed Henry VI. The usurpation of the Yorkist Richard III was terminated by Henry of Richmond, who was descended in the female line from an illicit union of John of Gaunt.

Henry VII's marriage to Elizabeth of York, the Yorkist heiress, united the claims of York and Lancaster, gave England the Tudor dynasty and removed the threat of further dynastic warfare.

Henry IV

Born Bolingbroke Castle 1367. Ascended throne 1399 (usurper).
Reigned 14 years.
Son of John of Gaunt.
Married (i) Mary de Bohun (ii) Joan of Brittany.
Four sons, two daughters.
Died Westminster 1413, aged 46. Buried in Canterbury Cathedral.

'A scrambling and unquiet time' – so Shakespeare described the reign of the first Lancastrian king, Henry IV. The very nature of his accession, his usurpation of the throne when there were others with a better title, created problems for the future. From 1399 to about 1410 Henry was never free from rebellions.

Richard II's half brothers rose immediately on his behalf. The rising was put down severely, and in 1400 Richard's body was exhibited in London to disprove a rumour that he was still alive.

From 1401, Owain Glyndŵr kept up a continuous guerrilla warfare against the Marcher lords, capturing Lord Grey and Sir Edward Mortimer in the following year. Both married daughters of Glyndŵr and formed with him, the disaffected Harry Percy (Hotspur) and Douglas from Scotland, a league against Henry. At Shrewsbury in 1403 they were routed and Hotspur killed, but two years later the Earl of Northumberland, the Duke of York and the Archbishop of York attempted another rebellion. They were foiled and the Archbishop and other rebels executed. A third revolt by Northumberland was defeated in 1408 at Bramham Moor, near Tadcaster, when the Earl was killed. There was no further outbreak of civil war until 1455.

During the last years of his reign Henry was a sick man, suffering from epileptic fits which encouraged his son Prince Hal to take over the reins of government, ousting the king's Chancellor, Thomas Arundel, Archbishop of Canterbury. The king, who had dreamed of going on a Crusade, died in the 'Jerusalem' Chamber in the house of the Abbot of Westminster in 1413.

Henry V

Born Monmouth 1387. Ascended throne 1413. Reigned 9 years.
Son of Henry IV.
Married Catherine of Valois.
One son.
Died Vincennes 1422, aged 35. Buried at Westminster.

Henry V, pious, stern and a skilful soldier after years spent fighting the Welsh, succeeded his father at the age of twenty-six. His magnanimity was immediately demonstrated by freeing the young Earl of March, a contender for the throne, and restoring to Hotspur's son his father's estates. Though he had to crush a conspiracy to further the Earl of March's claim and suppress Lollardy, Henry's reign was dominated by his renewal of the Hundred Years War. In doing so, he diverted England's attention away from possible internal discord: the nobles and their followers were anxious for war; Henry was equally anxious that they should not remain idle in England, and convinced himself that his cause was just, even pressing a claim to the French Crown through his great-grandfather, Edward III, whose mother was Philip IV's daughter. Despite some misgivings, Parliament voted money for the campaigns, and the Church was appeased by the king's continued persecution of the Lollards.

Henry was more successful in the French war than Edward III at his best, and succeeded in mastering northern France. In this he was assisted by an alliance with the Duke of Burgundy and the Emperor Sigismund, who visited England in 1416. Henry's army sailed from Southampton in 1415, using 1,500 ships to convey 8,000 troops and their equipment. Agincourt (1415), won in the face of tremendous odds and at a cost of 500 casualties to the French's 7,000, was only a stepping-stone to the Treaty of Troyes (1420). By the terms of this treaty – achieved with the aid of a disaffected group within

Opposite: Henry V: artist and date unknown *(The National Portrait Gallery, London)*.

47

France – Charles VI, the lunatic king of France, gave his daughter Catherine in marriage to Henry, and recognized him as his heir in preference to his own son, the Dauphin. Had he lived two months longer Henry V would, in theory, have been crowned King of France. In practice, however, the unconquered parts of France would never have accepted the treaty, and it is unlikely that Henry would have been able to assume the French crown without the complete conquest of the country. Given growing disquiet in England at his parlous financial position, it is doubtful whether he could have found the enormous sums required to fund such a campaign.

But Henry died suddenly of dysentery in 1422, leaving to his baby son a claim to the French throne that would be difficult to uphold, and a nobility in England that had gained practice in the business of warfare. The son was to reap the harvest of his father's policy.

Henry VI

Born Windsor Castle 1421. Ascended throne 1422. Reigned 1422–61 and 1470–1, 40 years.
Son of Henry V.
Married Margaret of Anjou.
One son.
Died London 1471 (murdered), aged 50. Buried (i) Chertsey Abbey (ii) Windsor (iii) ? Westminster.

Henry VI came to the throne in 1422, aged nine months. Within two months, on the death of Charles VI, he was also nominally king of France, though the Dauphin assumed the title. For the first twenty years of Henry's reign the government of England and the conduct of the inevitable war with France were in the hands of his quarrelsome uncles and cousins.

At first the progress of the war continued the successes of Henry V: the able Duke of Bedford won a victory at Cravant in 1423 and the following year the Dauphin's army was almost annihilated at Verneuil. The lack of funds and leaders as capable as Bedford to prosecute the war helped Joan of Arc to reverse English fortunes in 1428, when she relieved the desultory siege of Orléans. Even when she was captured and handed over to the English in 1430, she had revived French morale sufficiently for others to continue the reconquest of English territories, particularly after Burgundy's change of sides. When the Hundred Years War at last ended in 1453, Calais was all that remained of Henry V's conquests. The French renaissance made Henry's coronation as French king in Paris in 1431 seem an absurd gesture. The loss of Normandy diminished still further the prestige of a government which was already noted for its incompetence. The Bishop of Chichester and the Duke of Suffolk were but two of the casualties of mob anger.

In England the reign of Henry VI witnessed the most acute phase of the Wars of the Roses. The weak government was unable to control the nobles, accustomed to fighting by the long French campaign. The two aristocratic factions represented by Edmund Beaufort, Duke of Somerset, and the heir presumptive, Richard, Duke of York, battled for supremacy but they left the mass of people unaffected. Peasants were gaining more freedom, and the merchant class more power.

In 1454 the king succumbed to the madness which was hereditary in his mother's family, and the Duke of York was appointed Regent. The king's recovery in 1455 was accompanied by the outbreak of open hostilities between the families of Lancaster and York at St Albans in 1458. The Yorkists triumphed and Somerset was killed, Henry VI was captured but treated with respect by York who resumed his Regency.

In 1459 a Lancastrian revival, directed by the queen, Margaret of Anjou, who was as vigorous as her husband was weak, saw the flight of York, and his chief supporter, Richard Neville, Earl of Salisbury, of the tremendously powerful Neville family. By 1460 the struggle had become so bitter that York had claimed the throne, but at the end of the year the Lancastrians routed the Yorkists at Wakefield. York and Neville were both slain. In the following year small firearms were used for the first time in English history at the second Battle of St Albans, where Margaret defeated the Earl of Warwick. It was the last real success for the Lancastrian cause. In 1461 Edward, the late Duke of York's eldest son, had himself crowned as Edward IV at Westminster Hall and hurried north to overtake the retreating Lancastrians; they met during a snowstorm at Towton, south west of York, where Margaret's forces were decisively defeated, compelling her to flee with Henry and their son to Scotland.

Neville's popular son, the Earl of Warwick and Salisbury (known as the 'kingmaker') continued the campaign against the indomitable Margaret in the north of England, terminating her struggle in 1464 and capturing Henry near Clitheroe, Yorkshire, in the following year. The most powerful noble in England, Warwick fell out with Edward when the king, in the midst of Warwick's negotiations with France for a suitable marriage, announced that he was already married to Elizabeth Woodville, a Lancastrian widow and a commoner at that. Warwick was further angered by the advancement of the Woodville relations. His influence lost, Warwick intrigued with the French king, Louis XI, and at his insistence with the exiled Margaret of Anjou. Having been at war with her for years, this was not an easy condition to meet, but ultimately Warwick's youngest daughter Anne was married to Margaret's only son, Edward, Prince of Wales. In 1470 an invasion led by Warwick succeeded in releasing the mad Henry VI from the Tower and restoring him to a puppet's throne.

Edward fled to Burgundy, only to return in 1471. In two battles in that year Edward regained the throne. Warwick paid the price for trying to perform the function of

Henry VI: artist and date unknown *(The National Portrait Gallery, London)*.

kingmaker to both sides, at Barnet. Henry VI's son, Prince Edward, was killed at Tewkesbury, extinguishing the hopes of the Lancastrians who lost many leaders in the battle or through subsequent execution. After Tewkesbury Henry VI was killed, probably by Edward IV's brother, Richard, Duke of Gloucester, of later and greater infamous memory.

Edward IV

Born Rouen 1442. Reigned 1461–70 and 1471–83, 21 years.
Son of Richard, Duke of York.
Married Elizabeth Woodville.
Two sons, five daughters.
Died Westminster 1483, aged 41. Buried at Windsor.

Raised as the Earl of March, Edward proved to be a far more efficient statesman and soldier than the tragic Henry VI had been. But his morals were poor, disapproved of even by his not very particular contemporaries, and his greed was inordinate. His instruction to murder Henry VI's son Prince Edward and later his own brother Clarence while incarcerated in the Tower, together with his brutal treatment of captives, revealed his cruel ruthlessness. The nobles also took exception to his marriage to the daughter of Earl Rivers, compounded by the liberality with which Edward showered her family with favours.

After the death of Edward's father at the Battle of Wakefield in 1460, the Yorkist cause was revived by victory at Mortimer's Cross (1461), west of Ludlow. Although defeated at the second Battle of St Albans in the same year, Edward took advantage of Henry VI's plea to his victorious queen not to allow her wild levies to have the run of London, to enter the city and be crowned king. During the first part of his reign (see above), Edward's position on the throne was tenuous, having alienated his supporter Warwick and having to deal with rebellions fomented by Louis XI.

When Edward was compelled to flee to Flanders, he acquired an interest in literature and printing, encouraging him later to establish a book collection (now in the British Library) and to become patron to William Caxton who returned to England in 1476 after an absence of thirty-five years. Caxton established a printing-press at Westminster from which he issued a stream of books, many of them translated from Latin and French by himself.

The battles at Barnet and Tewkesbury put an end to the insecurity of the first part of his reign. He stimulated trade and strengthened control of the Welsh and Scottish borders, the last through his brother Richard whom he made 'King's Lieutenant in the North'. He also revived the old claim to the French throne and invaded France in alliance with his brother-in-law the Duke of Burgundy. At Picquigny in 1475 Louis XI paid 75,000 crowns and promised an annuity of 20,000 if Edward would return to England. Edward was able to live on this money and the proceeds from confiscated Lancastrian estates for the rest of his reign.

Edward's sudden death in 1483, worn out by a debauched life, was to lead to tragedy for his two sons, aged twelve and nine.

Edward V

Born Westminster 1470. Ascended throne 1483. Reigned 2 months.
Elder son of Edward IV.
Died London 1483 (?murdered). ?Buried at Westminster.

Twelve-year-old Edward V succeeded his father in April 1483. At the time he was at Ludlow Castle, and was dispatched to London with a small retinue that included two Woodville uncles. His mother had wanted an armed escort, but was refused it. *En route,* they were intercepted at Northampton by Edward's uncle Richard, Duke of Gloucester, who arrested the Woodville uncles and had the king lodged in the palace part of the Tower. Elizabeth hurried her second son, the Duke of York, and all her daughters into the sanctuary of Westminster Abbey. Yet for reasons that will always remain a subject for conjecture, she released her second son, perhaps to keep her brother company now that the date of coronation had been fixed, perhaps because she had been persuaded that sanctuary could not apply to children incapable of crime. Both sons disappeared.

Basing his claim on the grounds that Edward's marriage to Elizabeth Woodville was invalid, and that his children were therefore illegitimate, Gloucester seized the throne as Richard III.

The story of Richard's probable murder of his nephews is well known. In 1674, the skeletons of two children were discovered during alterations in the Tower and subsequently interred in Westminster Abbey.

Richard III

Born Fotheringay Castle 1452. Ascended throne 1483 (usurper). Reigned 2 years.
Son of Richard, Duke of York, and brother of Edward IV.
Married Anne Neville. One son.
Died Bosworth 1485, aged 33. Buried at Greyfriars Church, Leicester.

When he came to the throne in 1483 Richard was already credited with personal responsibility for the deaths of Henry VI, Henry's son and his own brother Clarence. Contemporaries, and posterity, were to saddle him with the murder of his two nephews, though his guilt is still questionable. Richard, Duke of Gloucester, had proved himself an able soldier and administrator, especially in the North. His nephew's youth, and the unpopularity of the Queen Mother's Woodville relations, might have seen England fall prey once again to internal wars. So Richard III's seizure of the throne in 1483 can be defended on the doubtful grounds of 'reasons of State'.

But the murder of his nephews and the ruthless extinction of anyone who opposed his will made his rule unpopular and set afoot many plots for vengeance. The first was led by his erstwhile collaborator, the Duke of Buckingham, who began treating with Henry Tudor, Earl of Richmond, and the focus of the Lancastrian cause. The rising collapsed and Buckingham was executed. It is thought that the princes in the Tower were executed shortly after this revolt, though Richard's complicity has never been proved. None the less his almost inevitable knowledge of the deed split the Yorkist party and lost Richard further support.

Richard tried to bribe the Duke of Burgundy to surrender Henry from his exile in Brittany, almost with success. Henry Tudor could trace his descent in the female line from John of Gaunt's illicit union with Katherine Swynford, making Henry's mother the great-great-granddaughter of Edward III. With such ancestry he was the 'nearest thing to royalty the Lancastrian party possessed'.

In France he gathered a small army, Lancastrian veterans and others anxious to see the end of Richard flocking to his support. Besides Richard's ruthlessness, his reliance on Northerners (understandable as he had spent much of his life in the North of England) antagonized people in the South. Henry landed at Milford Haven on 7 August 1485 and more men joined him. On 22 August at Market Bosworth in Leicestershire, the last important battle of the Wars of the Roses was fought. Richard III was killed in battle, and Richmond became king as Henry VII.

The marriage of Henry VII to the Yorkist heiress, Elizabeth of York, united the claims of Lancaster and York and gave England the Tudor line of monarchs. This remarkable woman was the daughter of Edward IV, sister of Edward V, niece of Richard III, wife of Henry VII, and mother of Henry VIII; she was also Queen of Scotland and of France.

Above: Edward IV: artist and date unknown *(The National Portrait Gallery, London)*.

Opposite: Richard III: artist and date unknown *(The National Portrait Gallery, London)*.

PART TWO

TUDORS
AND STUARTS

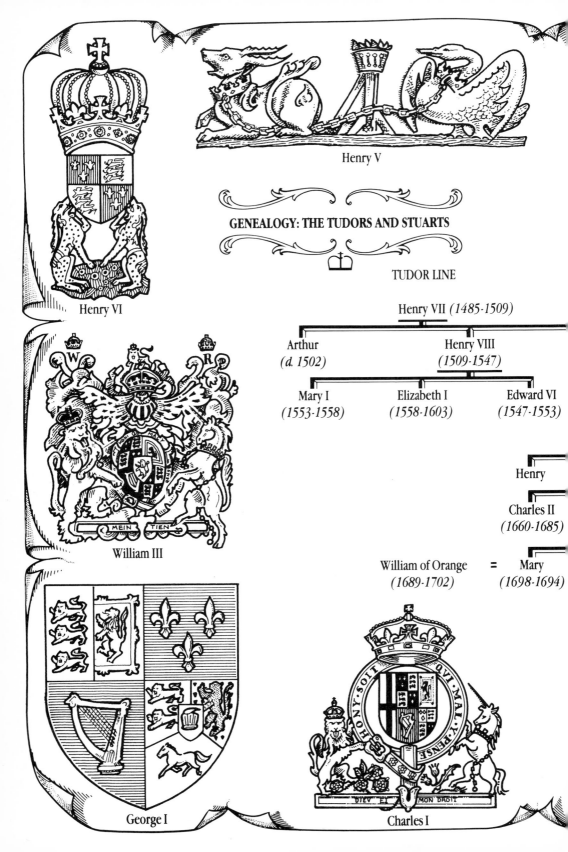

Henry V

GENEALOGY: THE TUDORS AND STUARTS

TUDOR LINE

Henry VII *(1485-1509)*

Arthur *(d. 1502)*

Henry VIII *(1509-1547)*

Mary I *(1553-1558)*

Elizabeth I *(1558-1603)*

Edward VI *(1547-1553)*

Henry

Charles II *(1660-1685)*

William of Orange *(1689-1702)* = Mary *(1698-1694)*

Henry VI

William III

George I

Charles I

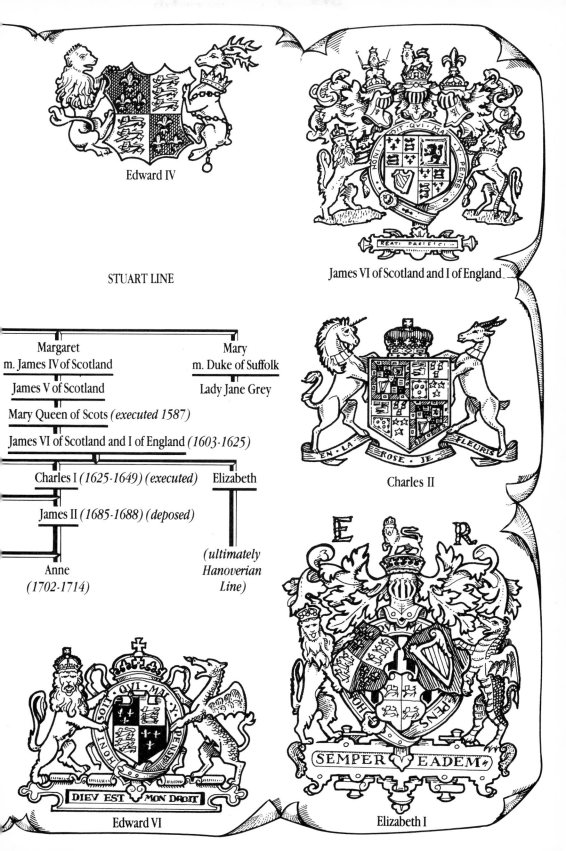

Edward IV

STUART LINE

James VI of Scotland and I of England

Margaret	Mary
m. James IV of Scotland	m. Duke of Suffolk
James V of Scotland	Lady Jane Grey

Mary Queen of Scots *(executed 1587)*

James VI of Scotland and I of England *(1603-1625)*

Charles I *(1625-1649) (executed)*   Elizabeth

James II *(1685-1688) (deposed)*

(ultimately Hanoverian Line)

Anne
(1702-1714)

Charles II

Edward VI

Elizabeth I

THE TUDORS

Henry VII

Born Pembroke Castle 1457 (his mother was 14 years old).
Ascended throne 1485. Reigned 24 years.
Son of Edmund Tudor.
Married 1486, Elizabeth of York, eldest daughter of Edward IV.
Two sons, two daughters.
Died Richmond 1509, aged 52 years. Buried at Westminster Abbey.

As victor at the Battle of Bosworth, where Richard III was killed, Henry Tudor ascended the throne in 1485. By his marriage in 1486 with the Yorkist heiress he finally ended the Wars of the Roses. Though the Tudor dynasty began in treason and bloodshed, it eventually brought a new, more peaceful era.

Henry was determined to restore order to the nation. By wise and firm – if sometimes avaricious – government, the old, fierce struggle between Crown and barons was ended. By heavy taxes and fines for misdemeanours, he impoverished the nobles and brought them to heel. The transitional period between the Middle Ages and Renaissance was bridged.

Henry's claim to the throne was weak, so it was not surprising that his position was challenged by pretenders and the disaffected. Lord Lovel in 1486 was followed by Lambert Simnel who was put forward as Clarence's son, Edward Plantagenet, the true Earl of Warwick; a baker's son, Simnel was crowned Edward VI in Dublin, but his forces met with little support in England and were crushed at Stoke, near Newark. The real Edward was released from prison by Henry to be paraded through the streets of London, and it was in Henry's kitchens that the captured Simnel was put to work.

More serious was the pretence by the Flemish Perkin Warbeck to be Richard, Duke of York, who was presumed murdered in the Tower: Warbeck was acknowledged as her nephew by Margaret, Edward VI's sister, and received by James IV of Scotland as the Duke of York. However, his invasion of the south west in 1498 was easily defeated and Warbeck executed after attempting to escape from the Tower. Another insurrection was prompted by the heavy taxation imposed by Henry; ill-armed Cornish miners and peasants marched on London and were within sight of the city before they were defeated.

To help counter threats arising from his poor claim to the throne, Henry sought to secure his position by dynastic marriages, though acceptance of his offers implied a tacit recognition of the likelihood of his holding the Crown: his eldest son Arthur was married to the Spanish princess Catherine of Aragon, and his daughter Margaret to King James IV of Scotland.

Henry sought peace in preference to pressing territorial claims in France, and after brief hostilities concluded the lucrative Treaty of Etaples with Charles VIII. Like the Treaty of Picquigny, it had a beneficial effect on commerce which was encouraged through trade agreements with Denmark, Florence and the Low Countries. In 1496 John Cabot was sent on the expedition which discovered Nova Scotia and Newfoundland; shipbuilding was encouraged with subsidies, and a start was made on establishing the navy.

Henry died exhausted by work. His attention to detail was legendary: he examined his accounts daily and bequeathed his personal fortune of £1½ million to his second son Henry who succeeded without opposition.

During Henry's reign, playing cards were first invented (1486): the portrait of his wife, Elizabeth of York, has appeared eight times on every deck of playing cards for over 500 years.

Henry VIII

Born Greenwich 1491. Ascended throne 1509. Reigned 38 years.
Second son of Henry VII.
Married six times.
One son, one daughter, by first wife; one daughter by second wife; one son by third wife.
Died Whitehall 1547, aged 56 years. Buried at Windsor.

The best-known fact about Henry VIII is that he had six wives, which has often been presented as a reflection of his lust. In fact it had far more to do with his concern to produce as trouble-free a succession as he had enjoyed. The inability of successive wives to produce a male heir spurred him to dispose of wives by whatever means were necessary:

Catherine of Aragon (widow of Henry's brother Arthur) – divorced.
Anne Boleyn (mother of Elizabeth I) – beheaded.
Jane Seymour (mother of Edward VI) – died.
Anne of Cleves – divorced.
Catherine Howard – beheaded.
Catherine Parr – outlived the king.

Above: Henry VIII: after Holbein, c1536 *(The National Portrait Gallery, London).*

Opposite: Henry VII: artist Michiel Sittow, painted in 1505 aged 48 *(The National Portrait Gallery, London).*

Although Henry seems to have married Catherine of Aragon partly because he could not repay her dowry to Arthur, their marriage was happy, and only the death of their son after a few days, followed by a series of miscarriages and still births drove Henry to seek a more fruitful union. After giving birth to Princess Elizabeth and a miscarriage, Anne Boleyn was accused of incest and adultery, and beheaded along with the brother she is supposed to have bedded. Jane Seymour died giving birth to Prince Edward, and the marriage to the physically disappointing Anne of Cleves was annulled on the grounds of non-consummation. Catherine Howard's previous attachments were the pretext for an accusation of adultery that led to her death in the Tower. Catherine Parr had been married twice before, and her maturity and ability to get on with Henry's children doubtless helped her to survive Henry.

In his early manhood Henry was accounted the most handsome and accomplished prince of his time, skilled both in learning and athletics. Unlike his father, he was ambitious for military glory. Three years after becoming king, he invaded France in his capacity as a member of the Holy League; he commanded the English with Austrian mercenaries, and won a rather insignificant cavalry action that had to be dignified by the name 'Battle of the Spurs'. In his absence the Scots invaded England and were decisively beaten by Lord Surrey at Flodden Field. James IV, Henry's brother-in-law, was killed and the flower of the Scots nobility slain.

Like many monarchs before him, Henry was soon seduced away from the *minutiae* of State affairs by the attractions of hunting and jousting, for both of which he held a passion, and by his demanding relationships in and out of wedlock. The growing willingness to leave the burden of government to his ministers enabled the three principal advisers of his reign, Thomas Wolsey, Thomas More and Thomas Cromwell, to exercise exceptional powers. Wolsey, a butcher's son from Ipswich, became one of the most powerful ministers in English history, living on a grand scale and owning two palaces – York Palace and Hampton Court – that surpassed even the king's own houses; in 1515 Henry compelled him to hand over Hampton Court. State occasions were invested with the same extravagance: at an inconsequential meeting in 1520 between Henry and Francis I of France, known as the Field of the Cloth of Gold, Wolsey was attended by 300 servants and set up fountains filled with wine. It was Wolsey's failure to arrange for Henry's divorce from his first wife that led to his dismissal in 1529 and summons the following year to London on a charge of high treason; he died on the journey.

Cromwell inherited Wolsey's problems, and the obduracy of the Pope over the question of a divorce forced him to draw up ever more radical plans to achieve Henry's desires. Using the law of *praemunire* to accuse the clergy of treason, Cromwell extracted from them a recognition of Henry's position as Supreme Head of the Church of England. An attack on papal finances was followed by the declaration by the new

Archbishop of Canterbury, Thomas Cranmer, that Henry's marriage was invalid. Excommunication by the Pope led to a flurry of Parliamentary legislation that sealed the break with Rome: an act in restraint of appeals declared invalid any pronouncements from Rome, and Acts of Submission, Succession and Supremacy confirmed Henry's position as head of the Church.

Henry's anti-papal campaign did not end there. The Dissolution of the Monasteries began in 1536. Henry's costly foreign policy had already drained the resources inherited from his father, making attractive the idea of confiscating the extensive estates attached to the monasteries. Another reason for the spoliation was that, if left undisturbed, they would be hotbeds for Catholic propaganda against Henry's break with the Papacy. The monks were indeed vulnerable to attack at this time, far too many of them being idle and immoral. Wolsey had begun the work by closing 29 communities of less than 7 inmates, devoting the revenues to his educational foundations in Oxford and Ipswich. In dissolving the monasteries, Cromwell brought to an end a major element in English life that went back almost a thousand years, and in so doing wrought the most dramatic redistribution of land since William I. The wealth assumed by the Crown was partly frittered away on a futile expedition to France that required a massive army of 40,000 men for the single gain of Boulogne.

The break with Rome was not concerned with altering doctrine: the Statute of the Six Articles confirmed the fundamental tenets of the Church of Rome, and allowed for dire penalties if ignored; and in 1537 Henry ordered the publication of the *Bishops' Book* or the *Institution of a Christian Man*, a conservative and orthodox tract except on the issue of the supremacy of the Pope. Henry himself wrote a book on the Sacraments in reply to Luther, for which he had received the title of 'Defender of the Faith' from the Pope, a title since borne by all his successors.* His full title was By the Grace of God, King of England, France and Ireland; the Supreme Head and Sovereign of the Most Noble Order of the Garter.

Opposition to the suppression of the monasteries was compounded by the beginnings of the enclosure movement, which deprived peasants of residual feudal rights to common land and, in converting arable land to pasture, reduced employment. It was most strongly felt in the North, where the Pilgrimage of Grace of 1536-7 drew its main support. Neither papist nor anti-Henry, the rising was conservative in its inspiration and aimed at persuading Henry to dismiss the detested Cromwell and to save the monasteries as the main source of alms for the poor. With false promises the Duke of Norfolk pacified and disarmed the rebels before beginning his savage retribution which included hanging and quartering the ringleaders. Abbots who

---

*The title is still to be found on current British coinage, in the forms Fidei Defensor, Fidei Def., Fid. Def., or just F.D.

supported the Pilgrimage or denied the royal supremacy were hung or executed.

Henry carried on his father's work of creating an effective navy. He built the *Great Harry,* of 1,000 tons, then the largest ship ever known; the first dockyard was created at Portsmouth, in 1540, and the navy was separated from the army for the first time. At his death, Henry had added some eighty ships to naval strength and so began the challenge to the maritime supremacy of Spain. A constitutional monarch in name, Henry was in reality all but absolute, and the question of Tudor despotism has provided fertile ground for historical debate. But in spite of the almost summary execution of wives, ministers and clergy, Henry was popular with the people throughout his reign and was a brilliant statesman; at a time when Europe was in turmoil, he maintained order without an army.

Edward VI

Born Hampton Court 1537. Ascended throne 1547. Reigned 6 years.
Son of Henry VIII and his third wife, Jane Seymour.
Unmarried.
Died 1553, aged 15 years. Buried Westminster Abbey.

Edward was nine years of age when he became king, and the reasons for Henry's anxiety about a weak succession became apparent: a weak child, he was never to exercise the authority of a king, dying of tuberculosis at fifteen. Edward's uncle, Edward Seymour, Earl of Hertford, was named Protector and virtually ruled the country, though with more humane methods than Henry.

He began by invading Scotland to enforce a marriage agreement between Edward and Mary, Queen of Scots, and defeated the Scots army at Pinkie. Soon created Duke of Somerset, Seymour with Archbishop Cranmer pushed further the religious revolution: John Knox, Ridley, Latimer and Hooper were appointed Court Preachers; Cranmer's beautifully written Book of Common Prayer (1549) was introduced to bring uniformity of worship and contributed to England's move towards becoming a Protestant state; the Six Articles (see page 65) were repealed along with Henry's heresy and treason laws. The debate over the Eucharist and the introduction of Cranmer's Prayer Book on Whit Sunday 1549 sparked a rebellion in parts of Devon and Cornwall, and in Norfolk, led by Robert Ket, resulting in bloody suppression and the fall of Somerset.

John Dudley, Earl of Warwick – a schemer with unbridled ambition – replaced Somerset as the leading noble in Council, and gradually introduced Edward into its affairs. The office of Protector was abolished, Warwick acting as Lord President of the Council. To help to restore order in the country, the office of Lord Lieutenant was created, charged with the preservation of peace in each shire. Soon made Duke of

Edward VI: after Holbein, c1542 *(The National Portrait Gallery, London)*.

Northumberland, Dudley hastened the pace of religious reform, introducing a second Book of Common Prayer. Northumberland mismanaged the country's already bad economy: prices were soaring, and hardship was keenly felt among the poor. He was more concerned, however, to secure the succession for his family, and to that end he married his fourth son, Lord Guildford Dudley, to Lady Jane Grey, who had a claim to be Edward's heir. Edward nominated in his will Lady Jane Grey as his successor, excluding his half-sisters, Mary and Elizabeth.

Edward died in the seventh year of his reign, leaving the country torn by opposing factions

Lady Jane Grey

Born Bradgate, Leicestershire 1537. Ascended throne 1553. Reigned 9 days.
Daughter of Henry Grey, Duke of Suffolk and Lady Frances Brandon.
Executed Tower Green 1554, aged 17 years.

At Edward's death, the next in succession was his sister Mary. But Northumberland, anxious for his family's advancement, persuaded the dying Edward to exclude Mary from the throne on the grounds of religion – she was a staunch Catholic. Lady Jane's claim to the throne was through her mother, who was daughter of Princess Mary by Charles Brandon, Duke of Suffolk. By Jane's unwilling marriage to Northumberland's son, her fate was yoked to his father's ability to press her claim. His unpopularity sealed their fate.

Though Council recognized her claim and instructions for her proclamation were sent out, only two towns responded. When Mary raised her standard at Framlingham and called on all supporters of the Tudor dynasty to rally to her cause, she received many pledges of help. Northumberland's troops, at Cambridge *en route* to Framlingham to arrest Mary, melted away and the Councillors did a volte-face and proclaimed Mary queen.

Lady Jane, her husband and Northumberland were prisoners in the Tower by the time Mary entered London in triumph in August 1553. Lady Jane refused to foresake Protestantism and scorned Northumberland for his craven recantation, which failed to save his life. None the less Mary might have spared her but for Wyatt's rebellion in opposition to Mary's rule and her proposed marriage to Philip of Spain. Lady Jane was beheaded on Tower Green in February 1554.

Mary I ('Bloody Mary')

Born Greenwich Palace 1516. Ascended throne 1553. Reigned 5 years.
Daughter of Henry VIII and his first wife, Catherine of Aragon.
Married Philip II of Spain.
No issue.
Died St James's Palace 1558, aged 42. Buried at Westminster Abbey (no monument).

Mary as the daughter of Catherine of Aragon had suffered an appalling childhood after her parents' divorce when she was ten. The subsequent neglect, persecution and ill-health obviously had their effect in the later days of her reign. In 1532 Mary and her mother parted, and Henry forbade Mary to see her mother even when Catherine was dying at Kimbolton. The following year Mary was declared illegitimate by Act of Parliament, and under great pressure she finally submitted to acknowledge Henry's supremacy and her own illegitimacy. After Edward's succession, a new kind of persecution began with attempts to make her abjure the mass. Like her mother she was to remain a devout Catholic. Her adherence to principle as the foremost guide to action helps to explain why her last years won her the appellation 'Bloody'.

She was thirty-seven years of age when she entered London as queen and exercised leniency towards Lady Jane and her husband. Only Northumberland and two accomplices were executed. Nor did she embark on a precipitate assault on all aspects of the Reformation in England. Rather she allowed Protestants who did not wish to live under a Catholic ruler to leave the country; they included four of Edward's bishops and some 800 who formed a Protestant Church of England in exile. Equally she was made well aware that the aristocracy and gentry would not tolerate an attempt to recover the monastic lands they had been given or bought. But the undoing of Cranmer's work was her priority and it began in 1553 when Parliament reluctantly passed the first Statute of Repeal. Priests who had taken wives were the first target. Catholic bishops, doctrines and practice were restored, and the papal legate, Mary's cousin Cardinal Pole, formally absolved the realm for its act of schism.

Her early marriage was considered essential and the Earl of Devon was the English candidate, but she chose instead her cousin, heir to the Spanish throne, the future Philip II who was already a widower and eleven years her junior. The Commons, realizing such a match would be the greatest threat to English independence since the days of Henry III, begged the queen to reconsider, but the consolidation of the Catholic religion in England was undoubtedly her aim, and she stood firm. Trouble broke out almost immediately with the rebellion led by Sir Thomas Wyatt who had hopes of simultaneous uprisings throughout England and the promise of French support. Neither materialized, though Wyatt reached Ludgate in the City of London, and only

Above: Mary I: artist, Master John, painted in 1544 aged 28 *(The National Portrait Gallery, London)*.

Opposite: Lady Jane Grey (Lady Dudley): attrib. Master John, c1545 *(The National Portrait Gallery, London)*.

Mary's personal plea in the Guildhall for the citizens of the capital to support her prevented the city falling to the rebels. Over a hundred executions followed, and Elizabeth was imprisoned on suspicion of complicity. The rising defeated, Philip came to England in 1554 and the marriage took place at Winchester the following year. Philip was to leave after only fourteen months, partly because of Mary's inability to conceive.

Mary surrounded herself with zealous Catholic advisers and then attempted to enforce the wholesale conversion of England. In the succeeding years she earned her title 'Bloody' Mary: Protestant bishops Latimer and Ridley and the sixty-seven-year-old Archbishop Cranmer were amongst those burnt at the stake. (The spot is marked by a bronze cross set into the roadway at Broad Street, Oxford.) The revival of the heresy laws led to the burning at the stake of almost 300 men and women, the overwhelming majority from the lower levels of English society. Few gentlemen who had been advocates of Protestantism under Edward VI were martyred, and it was this rather than the cruelty of burning that damaged the esteem in which the monarchy was held. The fires served only to rally more Englishmen to the Protestant faith.

Calais, which had been an English possession since 1347, was lost to France in 1558 after Mary had agreed to support the Emperor's struggle against France. Almost the only contribution to Elizabeth's inheritance was Mary's reform of finance and improvements to the roads, of which Elizabeth was to take full advantage.

Mary, after a life which had been one long tragedy, died in 1558.

Elizabeth I

Born Greenwich Palace 1533. Ascended throne 1558. Reigned 44 years.
Daughter of Henry VIII and his second wife, Anne Boleyn.
Unmarried.
Died Richmond 1603, aged 70. Buried at Westminster Abbey.

Elizabeth, the last of the Tudors, found England in a sad state when she ascended the throne. It was torn by religious fears and differences; Calais, last foothold on the Continent, had been lost; the French king had one foot in Edinburgh. In addition, there were many who had doubts about her title to the throne, though her accession was uncontested: for Protestants it meant an end to persecution, and Catholics were aware that her religious beliefs were not held with the passion of Mary.

Elizabeth was a remarkable woman, noted for her learning, her reputed command of nine languages (which included Cornish, Irish and Welsh), sometimes wayward, often wise. She loved jewels and beautiful clothes, but had a hard, sceptical intellect, coupled with a total lack of fanaticism, which helped her steer a sensible and moderate course through the conflicts of her long reign.

From first to last she was undoubtedly popular with the people and received loyalty from her statesmen. She made progresses an art and an aspect of monarchy, spending several months each year visiting her noble subjects, who were sometimes brought near to ruin by the expense of entertaining the queen and her retinue. Many an extension to a country house was prompted by an impending visit. Apart from the ancillary purpose of giving the household at her palaces a chance to clean them thoroughly, their objective was to show the monarch to her subjects, and much ceremony attended her passage through towns.

Contributing to the lack of opposition to Elizabeth's accession was the fortunate predominance of women both in control of three important countries and as alternative claimants to the throne: Elizabeth, England; Mary, Queen of Scots, Scotland; and her mother-in-law, Catherine de Medici, was Regent for Charles IX of France.

From the outset Elizabeth showed moderately Protestant inclinations, undoing Mary's church legislation and reinstating her father's. In this her hand was forced by Pope Paul IV's insistence that she renounce all claim to the throne on account of her illegitimacy (the result of her father's marriage to Jane Seymour in 1536). As England was a fief of the Holy See (see page 34), the Pope claimed the right to dispose of the Crown. This compelled Elizabeth to establish the Anglican Church with its Thirty-nine Articles, Book of Common Prayer and the sovereign as its head.

Elizabeth did her utmost to avoid war, though her concern to maintain England's independence encouraged her to do anything she could to weaken any power that threatened it. But with the massacre of the Huguenots in France and the subsequent rise of the pro-Spanish and ultra-Catholic parties on the Continent, England felt insecure and an army went to the assistance of the French Protestants. After an initial reluctance to go to the support of rebels against a lawful sovereign, Elizabeth aided the Spanish Netherlands (present-day Belgium) in its struggle for independence from Spain. She also skilfully assisted the Protestant cause in Scotland when in the name of Protestantism the Scottish lords rebelled against the Catholic Regency of Mary of Guise, while her daughter Mary, Queen of Scots, lived in France with her husband the Dauphin. The Treaty of Edinburgh in 1560 enabled the Scottish Parliament to abolish the authority of the Pope in Scotland and to establish a Presbyterian form of Church.

It was an age of great adventurers and the queen undoubtedly had a genius for selecting capable advisers. Hawkins, Howard, Walsingham, the Cecils, Drake, Raleigh, Leicester, Essex, Burleigh, the Gilberts and many more made England both respected and feared. The disquiet caused by the massing of the Spanish Armada brought pressure on Elizabeth to allow Drake to attack Cadiz and in a brilliant action destroy the shipping ('singeing the King of Spain's beard', he called it). Catholic plots in support of Mary, Queen of Scots were repeatedly discovered, and after being beseeched by Parliament to execute her, Elizabeth acquiesced in 1587. When the Armada sailed in

1588 it was the largest expeditionary force known to history. Following on from Henry VIII's naval reforms, Sir John Hawkins had been equipping the navy with lighter and faster ships fitted with heavier, longer-range guns. Under the command of Lord Howard of Effingham, the English fleet harried the Armada up the Channel until Calais, where overnight Howard sent in eight fire-ships. They dispersed the Spanish and by a combination of fine captaincy by Drake, Hawkins and Frobisher, favourable weather patterns and superior navigational skills, a decisive victory was won, 44 of the 130 Spanish ships never returning to port.

Philip continued to attempt invasion with two further Armadas; both were defeated by the weather rather than English action, but it was in Ireland that he caused the greatest trouble with his support of Tyrone's rising in 1595. After inflicting a defeat on the English forces in 1597, Tyrone had an easy time of it in the face of the Earl of Essex's mixture of ineptitude and cowardice, which led to his downfall. Baron Mountjoy was sent to take over and defeated Tyrone and his 5,000 Spanish troops. Essex attempted a revolt in 1601, as ill-conceived as his Irish débâcle, and he was beheaded in the Tower.

During Elizabeth's reign England's progress in the field of discovery and colonization was tremendous. Raleigh's first Virginian colony was founded; Drake circumnavigated the globe, returning after a voyage of three years with £1½ million worth of treasure; the East India Company was founded, and English seamen left their mark in many parts of the world. Englishmen at this time were the lowest taxed in Europe.

Despite many suitors and offers of marriage, Elizabeth remained the only unmarried monarch of marriageable age since the Conquest. Part of her intention was not to diminish her authority or popularity, but also to prevent an alliance in support of the Counter-Reformation developing between France and Spain by protracting marriage negotiations with the French.

Elizabeth left the country secure, and religious troubles had largely disappeared. England was a first-class power. The queen proved herself particularly wise in statecraft, and though she held the Tudor view that the Crown had absolute supremacy over Parliament, she was tactful enough to avoid clashes between the two. The reign, too, was rich in learning: it was the age of Shakespeare, Sidney, Spenser, Bacon, Marlowe and many other famous names.

Opposite: Elizabeth I: artist unknown, c1575 *(The National Portrait Gallery, London).*

THE STUART KINGS

James I (VI of Scotland)

Born Edinburgh Castle 1566. Ascended throne 1603. Reigned 22 years.
Son of Mary, Queen of Scots and Henry, Lord Darnley.
Crowned King of Scotland as James VI, after his mother's abdication in 1567.
Married Anne of Denmark.
Three sons, four daughters.
Died Theobalds 1625, aged 59. Buried at Westminster Abbey.
First of the Stuarts.

James was born just three months after his mother's Court favourite had been butchered to death in an adjacent room. His whole childhood was pitiable, spent amid a turmoil of war, murder, plot and counter-plot, among as blood-thirsty a set of intriguers as could be found. His father was blown up when James was eight months old, and his mother married his murderer within a year, after which James was never to see her again. Within a few months of her remarriage, Mary was forced to abdicate and imprisoned at Lochleven.

James was crowned King of Scotland at Stirling, and though he made formal protests when his mother was executed in 1587 at Fotheringay, never showed any real feeling on the matter. In eleven years, four Regents exercised power, the first three coming to violent or suspicious ends. When sixteen, James was kidnapped by Lord Gowrie and held for eleven months. In 1589 he went to Christiania (now Oslo) to marry Anne of Denmark when he was twenty-three years of age and his bride fifteen. Though the marriage was somewhat lacklustre, it secured the succession with Prince Henry (1594) and Prince Charles (1600). During the 1590s, James gradually asserted control of the country, though there were repeated threats and the enigmatic Gowrie conspiracy, when an attempt was apparently made on James's life.

A Protestant, he was nevertheless engaged continually in intrigues with Rome up to the time of the death of Elizabeth, when he became James I of England and the first king to reign over both countries. Until then English and Scots had treated each other as foreigners, and James had a hard struggle to make the English take a milder attitude to Scotland. His journey south to assume the throne was something of a triumphal progress, during which he created over 300 knights and enjoyed the revels laid on for him at country houses *en route*.

James had a troubled reign. He ceaselessly preached 'the divine right of Kings', maintaining that the king was above the law; the House of Commons and the lawyers firmly opposed him, denying him money to pay his debts. He had high ideals, but he was no statesman, and his corrupt, ill-chosen favourites and extravagant Court aroused great animosity. So did his sale of titles which debased them and the Crown. Macaulay said of James: 'He was made up of two men – a witty, well-read scholar who wrote, disputed and harangued, and a nervous, drivelling idiot who acted.' Perhaps the most shameful episode of James's reign was his treatment of Sir Walter Raleigh, whom he offered to hand over to Philip III of Spain for execution after Raleigh's return from an ill-fated search for gold up the Orinoco River during which there had been a contretemps with the Spanish.

His first encounter with Parliament was an inept and tactless attempt to unify Scotland and England as Great Britain; it was coolly received by Parliament, so he introduced the name 'Britain'. It was the first of a series of conflicts that would lead ultimately to a king's execution, the Commons anticipating in the Apology of 1604 the deterioration into armed struggle: 'The privileges of the subject are for the most part at an everlasting stand . . . being once lost are not recovered but with much disquiet.'

In 1605 an attempt to blow up king and Parliament by Catholic sympathisers became known as the Gunpowder Plot. It failed, but brought a new wave of anti-Catholicism. The Puritans for their part were clamorous in their demands, challenging much of Elizabeth's Church settlement. Small religious groups found scant tolerance; in 1620 the Pilgrim Fathers sailed for America in their little ship *Mayflower,* seeking to found a community where their Calvinist tenets could flourish undisturbed. In 1611 the Authorised Version of the Bible was published, a landmark both for religion in England and for literature.

James's unproductive reign ended with the country close to war with Spain, partly due to the fiasco in which marriage negotiations for Charles ended. A cornerstone of James's foreign policy, such as it was, had been cordial relations with Spain; Charles and the royal favourite Buckingham had done much to undermine them in a madcap visit to Madrid in the expectation of securing the hand of the Infanta. They returned empty-handed and were urging the Commons into a bellicose position when James died. With the kingdom's finances in disarray and an antagonistic relationship between king and Commons, Charles inherited a delicate position.

Above: James I: after J. de Cutz the elder, date unknown *(The National Portrait Gallery, London)*.
Opposite: Charles I: artist, Daniel Mytens, painted in 1631 when aged 31 *(The National Portrait Gallery, London)*.

Charles I

Born Dunfermline 1600. Ascended throne 1625. Reigned 24 years.
Son of James I and Anne of Denmark.
Married Henrietta Maria of France.
Four sons, five daughters.
Died Whitehall 1649, aged 48 years (executed). Buried in Henry VIII vault, Windsor.

Charles was a weak, rickety child, unable to walk until seven or talk until five, after which he had a slight stammer. Though he grew up to be courageous, he lacked judgement, and his strong prejudices accompanied by the tactlessness common to the Stuarts were to prove his undoing.

Several attempts were made when Charles was in his teens to arrange marriages that would form alliances, and to this end he was eventually married to the Catholic Henrietta Maria, daughter of Henry IV of France. Though it was eventually a happy union, it did not begin auspiciously. The terms of the marriage articles permitted Henrietta Maria to exercise her religion and to be responsible for the upbringing of any children until they were thirteen. As this contravened an undertaking Charles had given to Parliament, the terms had to be secret; none the less Parliament got wind of them, which helped to foment suspicion arising from the queen's strong devotion to Catholicism. Her huge entourage angered many at Court, and within a year Charles had sent packing a bishop, 29 priests and 410 attendants. The queen's advice and faction were later to play a crucial role in moulding Charles's opinions.

Early in his reign Charles encountered difficulties with Parliament, for he stubbornly refused to accept dictation. Three times it was summoned and three times dissolved, until from 1629 for eleven years he governed by personal rule, known as the 'Eleven Years' Tyranny'. Without Parliament there was no money, and the Commons' mistrust had been illustrated by granting Charles tonnage and poundage for only one year, instead of the customary sanction for life. He needed money for simultaneous war with Spain and France, but Parliament was reluctant to supply it, fearing its incompetent use by Buckingham, who continued to be the royal favourite. Their scepticism was justified by the catastrophic raid on Cadiz when an admiral who had never before put to sea vainly tried to emulate Drake's brilliant exploit (see page 73). Buckingham and Charles had hoped the raid might furnish booty on an Elizabethan scale; instead they were reduced to attempting to pawn the crown jewels, selling monopolies, exploiting royal forests and the extension of 'ship money' to inland towns and shires.

Buckingham's murder in Portsmouth *en route* to the relief of La Rochelle did not end the mistrust between king and Parliament. Though Buckingham had been described as 'the great author of our misfortunes', his views closely reflected Charles's and the first meeting of Parliament without him, in 1629, ended in violence and the arrest of three Members. Though there was a strong case for assisting Protestant countries fighting for survival under a Catholic onslaught, Parliament's suspicion over the uses to which an army might be put by Charles precluded such action.

The eleven years during which Charles governed without Parliament were dominated by religious issues, and particularly the work of Archbishop Laud in trying to rein in the drift towards Puritanism, both by control and improving the quality of candidates for ordination. Laud's reforms alienated not only Puritans but even landowners whose social position and property were threatened. It was the desire for uniformity in imposing a new Scottish prayer book based on the English one that was to trigger off a sequence of events leading to civil war. Charles would probably never have recalled Parliament had not the rioting that greeted the prayer book's introduction led to the situation in Scotland getting out of control. When Charles saw in York the rag-tag army that the Earl of Essex had assembled to impose order on the Scots, he realized the need to recall Parliament to obtain subsidies. In the Commons John Pym insisted that grievances should be heard before any subsidies were voted; Charles refused to concede or listen to the counsel of his principal adviser, Wentworth, Earl of Strafford, and dissolved this Short Parliament.

The Scots, meanwhile, advanced over the Tweed and occupied Newcastle. The Treaty of Ripon (1640) provided for the Scots to remain in Northumberland and Durham and receive £850 a day until a settlement was reached. Parliament was recalled and met in militant mood: Strafford and Laud were impeached and sent to the Tower, and other royal officials fled. Though proof of the charges against Strafford could not be found, he was sacrificed by Charles and executed, shortly followed by Laud. The Long Parliament dismantled the king's prerogative and began an assault on episcopacy when the Irish began butchering the Protestant English who had been settled in Ireland. Again, the question arose of who would command the troops raised to restore order. Amidst deliberately spread rumours that the queen might be impeached, in January 1642 Charles planned a coup in which five particularly troublesome Members would be seized; forewarned they had left the House by a back door. A gradual polarization of positions led to the Nineteen Propositions, in which Parliament claimed a major extension of its powers. Two months later Charles raised his standard at Nottingham.

The king's strength lay broadly in the north and west and amongst conservative elements and Catholics. The Scots Covenanters sided with Parliament which, besides its strength in the south and east, controlled London, Hull, Plymouth, Bristol, Gloucester and Portsmouth. It is estimated that the parts of country controlled by Parliament contained some two-thirds of the population and three-quarters of the country's wealth.

The first part of the war was indecisive, the major battle at Edgehill illustrating only the superiority of the royalist cavalry. After the battle, Charles entered Oxford in triumph, making the city his headquarters for his intended move on London. The help of the Scots and the creation of the New Model Army by Fairfax and Oliver Cromwell proved decisive. Although there were royalist victories even in early 1645, and Montrose's brilliant diversions in Scotland on behalf of the king raised morale amongst royalists, the scale of their defeats at Marston Moor (1644) and Naseby (1645), followed by Rupert's loss of Bristol (which had earlier been won from the Parliamentarians), meant the end of Charles's military hopes. He left Oxford in disguise and made his way to the Scottish camp outside Newark where he gave himself up. When Charles refused to accept the Covenant, he was handed over to Parliament. Eventually, in 1648, he was arraigned before a tribunal consisting of 135 judges, but he refused to recognize the authority of the court and so would not plead. Sentence was passed by sixty-eight votes to sixty-seven, and by one vote Charles lost his head, being executed in Whitehall.

Oliver Cromwell

Born Huntingdon 1599. Virtual dictator 1653–8.
Died 1658, aged 59 years. Buried initially Westminster and after Restoration at Tyburn.

Oliver Cromwell was born into a moderately landed family with estates in Huntingdon and Cambridgeshire. Educated at Sidney Sussex College, Cambridge, where he imbibed Puritan thinking, he studied law in London before returning to farm the family lands.

When the troubles between Parliament and king began, Cromwell was an inconspicuous Member of Parliament. His puritanical fervour and passionate if clumsy oratory quickly led him to a position of eminence in the Commons. He had no military experience until his forty-fourth year at the first battle of the civil war where he was captain of a troop of horse. At Marston Moor his quick insight into the way the battle was developing and the strict training of his cavalry turned the course of the fighting and won the day.

Assuming the role of leader of the Independents (forerunners of today's Congregationalists), he pushed aside the more conservative generals like Manchester and created the New Model Army under Fairfax. After the victory at Naseby (1645), Cromwell negotiated with the king in the hope of reaching a settlement, but Charles's intrigues led Cromwell to denounce the king to the Commons as 'so great a dissembler and so false a man that he was not to be trusted'. Charles's machinations produced a Scots' invasion by Hamilton whose army Cromwell annihilated at Preston (1648).

In 1649, after Charles had been beheaded, Cromwell was given command in Ireland, where Royalist campaigns were still strong; he stormed Drogheda and Wexford,

Oliver Cromwell: after Robert Walker, date unknown *(The National Trust Photographic Library)*.

massacring the garrisons with a thoroughness that has left his name for ever notorious in Irish history; he alleged that the slaughter was 'the judgement of God' upon the people. The Puritans' Act of Settlement for Ireland showed a total absence of understanding of the country's needs.

Scotland, too, which was sheltering and supporting the young Prince Charles, had to be subdued. The battle against Leslie at Dunbar (1650) was at first close-run, but ended decisively. Cromwell occupied Edinburgh but illness laid him low for a year, during which time the Scots had reformed and moved south. Cromwell caught up with them at Worcester (1651) and ended royalist hopes, Charles II taking ship for France.

Cromwell became Lord General of the Commonwealth and then, in 1653, Lord Protector, a position which was a virtual dictatorship, even though in theory the nation was ruled by a Council of State, comprising seven army leaders and eight civilians. Cromwell lost patience with Parliament in much the same way as Charles had done, and used equally high-handed methods to obtain his objectives. England and Wales were divided into eleven districts with a Major-General over each. Scotland and Ireland were given representation in Parliament. Later Cromwell was offered the title of king, but republican sentiment in the army made him decline the suggestion.

Cromwell began a new foreign policy that restored the country's prestige and made the Commonwealth the head and protector of Protestant Europe. He made peace with Holland, concluded treaties with Denmark to reopen the Baltic to shipping and protect naval supplies, and hoped to expunge the humiliation of Cadiz (see page 80) by an alliance with France against Spain. Robert Blake took Jamaica, and after a blockade of the Spanish coast destroyed a Spanish treasure fleet in the bay of Santa Cruz. On land the Spanish were defeated at the Battle of the Dunes (1658) and Dunkirk was England's reward. Realizing the importance of the navy, Cromwell turned it into a full-time service with promotion structure and pay scales.

At home, Parliament was proving unable to cope with the country's chaotic condition. Its outlook was narrowly Puritan – far narrower than that of Cromwell himself in some ways; for instance severe penalties were laid down for travelling on Sunday or for profanity. The mass of the army, on whose support Parliament relied, disliked such measures; Cromwell was caught between the two, receiving much of the blame for the joyless, unsettled state of the country. A reaction set in against rule by the sword, and royalist plots and assassins threatened his life.

At his death he was buried with great pomp in Westminster Abbey, but at the Restoration his body was gibbeted at Tyburn and his head stuck on a pole outside Westminster Hall, remaining there for twenty years until it blew down in a gale. His body was buried at Tyburn and his head near the chapel at Sidney Sussex, Cambridge.

His son, Richard Cromwell, succeeded to his position, but was not a strong enough character to settle such a divided nation, nor to resolve the chronic financial problems bequeathed to him. Army and Parliament were unable to agree on a government, and the Restoration in 1660 was more or less a transaction between royalists and Puritans against the army – intended more as a Restoration of Parliament than of the king himself. Richard Cromwell had to go to France, but returned in 1680 and lived peaceably through four reigns, dying in 1712 at the age of eighty-six.

Charles II

Born St James's Palace 1630. Ascended throne 1660. Reigned 25 years.
Second son of Charles I and Henrietta Maria of France.
Married Catherine of Braganza.
No legitimate issue.
Died Whitehall 1685, aged 55 years. Buried at Westminster Abbey.

As a lad of twelve, Charles was with his father at the Battle of Edgehill, and when the Civil War was nearing its end he escaped to France. Later, he moved on to Holland, and in 1650 landed in Scotland, where he agreed to terms stipulated by the Commissioners; having subscribed to the Covenant he was crowned King of Great Britain, France and Ireland at Scone. A year later he marched into England with 10,000 men; when battle was joined with Cromwell's troops at Worcester, the Scottish army was overwhelmingly defeated. Charles, with a price of £1,000 on his head, was a fugitive for six weeks before he made his escape to France on a coal-brig from Shoreham.

He roamed Europe for nine years, continuously plotting and hoping for a royalist uprising. Richard Cromwell's weakness led to the dominance of the army, the dismantling of the Protectorate and Cromwell's resignation. A timely letter from Charles reassured Parliament of his intentions, should he be made king. With General Monck's influence, Charles was invited to return; on 29 May 1660, his thirtieth birthday, he arrived in a joyful London. The Restoration had been remarkably quick, and without detailed discussion over the king's position. But as a result, certain issues remained unresolved. Charles was still bound by the Covenant, but Parliament ordered it to be burned in 1661, passing an Act of Uniformity the following year that imposed Anglican doctrine. The Restoration gave Scotland back its independence, and episcopacy was reintroduced into the Kirk.

It was said of Charles that 'he never said a foolish thing and never did a wise one' but this overlooks his acute handling of several crises. He was intelligent, tolerant and much interested in scientific developments; if he submitted to working through a Parliament that was becoming a two-party system, Whig and Tory, it was as much because he preferred the pursuits of racing, hunting and women than that he conceded the need for a limitation on monarchical power. But then following Charles I, only a

Charles II: studio of Joseph Michael Wright, date unknown *(The National Portrait Gallery, London)*.

James II: artist Sir Peter Lely, date unknown *(The National Portrait Gallery, London)*.

fool would have allowed a repetition of his dealings with Parliament. Charles II's busy social life gave Edward Hyde, Earl of Clarendon, a free hand as High Chancellor until his exile in 1667 after being impeached due to his unpopularity.

It was the war with Holland, declared in 1665, that proved Clarendon's final undoing. The plague that year claimed 70,000 lives in London alone, naval funds were so depleted that many ships were laid up and sailors' pay in arrears. The following years France and Denmark joined the coalition against England. In 1667 a Dutch squadron sailed up the Thames estuary, burned English warships and towed away the flagship, the *Royal Charles*. Following on the heels of the Great Fire of London, which destroyed 13,000 houses the previous year, a scapegoat for the spate of disasters was needed and found in Clarendon, whom Charles made no effort to save.

Charles's 'foreign policy' has been the subject of much debate: though the sale of recently acquired Dunkirk (see page 84) for £400,000 angered the nation, the town was of little value without Calais or other strongholds to support it. But it was Charles's secret treaties with France that aroused the most suspicion; by the Treaty of Dover he even undertook to declare his personal Catholicism, and many doubted the wisdom of any agreement that bolstered further France's growing power. The return to war with Holland was without benefit. The failure to produce an heir raised the fear that, with the conversion to Catholicism of James, Duke of York, in 1669, England would again be faced with religious strife. This helped the nonsensical accusations by Titus Oates in the Popish Plot of 1678, whereby Jesuit priests were to murder the king, to gain an undeserved credence. Neither the facts nor the logic of Jesuit priests killing a Catholic-inclined king stand up to a second's scrutiny, but it raised all manner of further allegations throughout the country. Oates's accusations led the Opposition to try to force Charles to alter the succession, putting forward the Protestant Duke of Monmouth or William of Orange as candidates. But Charles would not sign an Exclusion Bill to forbid James's succession, and after the real treason of the Rye House Plot, in which a number of Whigs planned to kill Charles and his brother on their way back from Newmarket, Charles won the upper hand. James's accession was assured, and Charles died a Catholic, the priest who had helped him to escape from Worcester in 1651 being smuggled into his room to receive him into the faith.

After years of war and exile, Charles had hoped for an easier life: he married the Portuguese Catherine of Braganza in 1662, glad of her dowry of £300,000 with the naval bases of Tangier and Bombay; but he also had thirteen known mistresses, including Lucy Walters (mother of James, Duke of Monmouth), Barbara Villiers (later Countess of Castlemaine) and the famous Nell Gwynne, all of whom he treated with consideration. In all there were fourteen acknowledged illegitimate offspring. Of twenty-six dukes in England today, five are direct descendants on the wrong side of the blanket of Charles II. This applies to several marquesses and earls.

James II (VII of Scotland)

Born St James's Palace 1633. Ascended throne 1685. Reigned 3 years.
Third son of Charles I and brother of Charles II.
Married (i) Anne Hyde (ii) Mary of Modena.
Four sons, two daughters by first wife. Two sons, five daughters by second wife.
Died St Germain, Paris 1701, aged 68 years. Buried at St Germain, Paris.

Like his brother, James took part in the Civil War, and when exiled took service with the French and Spanish, respectively in Holland and Flanders, where he distinguished himself.

James developed a reverence for established institutions from his father-in-law, particularly for the Church but also for the law and the authority of Parliament. He expected advisers to have the same reverence for him, letting it be known that the way to his favour was 'to follow his wishes blindly, and to own an attachment to his interests that was without any qualification or reserve whatsoever'. Yet he saw concessions as a weakness, and significantly regarded the reason for Charles I's downfall not as obduracy but his giving any ground at all. James said he 'knew the English people and they could not be held to their duty by fair treatment'.

James had been converted to Catholicism in 1669 and admitted it openly when the Test Act was passed in 1673. The Act limited government offices to those who subscribed to the Anglican sacraments; James therefore had had to relinquish his position at the Admiralty. The violent anti-Catholic feeling which followed the Popish Plot in 1678 had made him very unpopular and he was persuaded by Charles II to go abroad; his brother, however, successfully thwarted attempts to exclude James from the succession. At the end of the following year, James returned, to be High Commissioner for Scotland.

Within six months of James's accession, another James, the Duke of Monmouth, illegitimate son of Charles II by Lucy Walters, landed at Lyme Regis, Dorset, and was proclaimed king by Protestant adherents at Taunton. A battle fought at Sedgemoor crushed the rebellion at a stroke. Monmouth was captured hiding in a ditch, the king refused a pardon and he was executed. The uprising was followed by the 'Bloody Assizes' of Judge Jeffreys (his 'campaign in the west' as James put it) when many hundreds of those who had taken part were transported for life. Some 230 were executed and many hundreds died in prison or were fined or flogged.

Religious persecution began on a large scale. James committed every stupid error that was possible: he heard mass in public, suspended the Test Act, bestowed ecclesiastical benefices on Roman Catholics, violated the rights of Oxford and Cambridge universities by imposing Catholic masters, intrigued with the French king

William III: after Sir Peter Lely, date unknown *(The National Portrait Gallery, London)*.

Mary II: after W. Wissing, date unknown *(The National Portrait Gallery, London)*.

(from whom, like his brother, he received a subsidy), packed Parliament with his supporters and crushed Protestantism. Ignoring even the advice of loyal Tories, he became a deeply loathed figure. Nor did the odd combination of piety and debauchery add to the regard in which he was held. By ignoring the lessons that could have been learned from his father's handling of Parliament, James lost the throne Charles had so tenaciously preserved for him.

In November 1688, William of Orange, who had married Mary, the daughter of James, landed at the head of 14,000 men at Brixham in Devon to start the 'Glorious Revolution'; he came at the invitation of seven aristocrats who assured William that the overwhelming majority of Englishmen would welcome him as a deliverer. At first the men of the west were slow to join William, having bitter memories of the Monmouth Rebellion, but as he neared the capital men of all parties rallied round simultaneous risings in Cheshire and Yorkshire, and even James's daughter Anne and her husband Prince George of Denmark went over to William's side.

James, in the months before William's landfall, tried to reverse some of his more disliked decisions, but to no avail; he had alienated all but a few Catholics and loyal Tories. Though James had plenty of warning of William's intentions and had made preparations to resist, James fled the country without a fight, leaving the throne vacant. Louis received James hospitably, lending him St Germain. He made an effort to regain the throne in 1689, but was heavily defeated at the Battle of the Boyne in Ireland and returned to France, where he died.

William III and Mary II

William:
Born The Hague 1650. Ascended throne 1689. Reigned 13 years.
Son of William II, Prince of Orange (of Holland) and Mary, eldest daughter of Charles I.
Died Kensington 1702, aged 52 years. Buried at Westminster Abbey.

Mary:
Born St James's Palace 1662.
Daughter of James II and Anne Hyde. No issue.
Died Kensington 1694, aged 32. Buried at Westminster Abbey.

William of Orange was the champion of the Protestant cause in Europe. After the murder of the Dutch leader De Witt, William was chosen to be the Stathouder of the United Provinces, then at war with France. William's military and diplomatic skills brought the war to an end with a treaty advantageous to the Netherlanders. He married Mary in 1677.

Given the circumstances of the invitation to invade England (see page 92), it is not surprising that William was enthusiastically received in London, though it was far from clear how the constitutional position would be resolved. William was in a strong position with so large an army of mercenaries, and he made it clear that he would not be happy with a Regency; he would accept the Crown or nothing. For Mary's part, despite an ostensibly cool marriage, she was devoted to William and would not think of ruling without him. Accordingly Parliament had little alternative but to offer them the Crown jointly as king and queen regnant, which they accepted and were crowned in 1689. Princess Anne, Mary's younger sister, reluctantly surrendered her place in the succession to William, who would thus have the Crown for life if Mary died before him; Mary did in fact die all too soon, of smallpox, in 1694.

The importance of the Glorious Revolution was that the monarchy became constitutional and Parliamentary; the fundamental struggles between Crown and Parliament were largely resolved, and arguably spared Britain the turmoil that overtook many European countries during the nineteenth century. William had been declared king by Parliament; the theory of the king as divinely ordained and set apart was finally dead. To prevent a recurrence of the Catholic revival under James, a Bill of Rights decreed that no Catholic or person with a Catholic spouse could be eligible to hold the Crown. But one area that continued to cause friction between Crown and Parliament was finance; Parliament was determined to retain its supply as a lever, and was deliberately parsimonious. Moreover, the pragmatic nature of William's return and settlement left other issues unresolved; perhaps chief amongst them was what was to become the perennial question of how much influence or control the monarch's ministers should have over Parliament, and how much say Parliament should have in the ministers' selection.

William was a brave, unfanatical king, respected though not loved by his people; there were even examples of unnecessarily cruel restrictions on his household that reflect ingratitude for helping to relieve the country of James II. His heart lay always with the Dutch and the desire to diminish French power. His wife Mary was more in favour, and helped win English loyalty until her early death.

A convention held in Scotland extended the English offer of the throne to William and Mary, provided they agree to abolish the episcopacy and institute Presbyterianism. Though a Calvinist, William was impartial on religious matters, and he worked hard to settle Scotland, where politics and religion were combining to produce a violent upheaval. James still had his adherents in the country, and the clans led by Viscount Dundee defeated William's troops under General Mackay at Killiecrankie in 1689; however, Dundee died of his wounds after the battle, and with him died James's cause in Scotland. The one blot on William's name was the Massacre of Glencoe in 1692, when a Highland clan, late in making submission to him, was almost obliterated.

Though the man who issued the order, the Secretary of State for Scotland, Sir James Dalrymple, was dismissed after a later inquiry, William gave him an indemnity and had himself signed the order, though whether he realized its import no one knows.

Jacobite plans to restore James to the throne haunted William's reign, the more dangerous being those outside the country. In 1689 James, fortified with French men and money, landed in Ireland, which was still held by the Irish Jacobite leader, the Earl of Tyrconnel. William himself headed an army of 36,000 men and decisively won the Battle of the Boyne; James fled to France for ever.

William soon had Britain, as part of a coalition of ten powers, at war with France, a war which went on ingloriously until 1697, when financial stress and diplomacy forced the allies to come to terms with their enemy.

The War of Spanish Succession, caused by the death in 1700 of the childless Charles II of Spain, brought a further menace from France; Philip, grandson of Louis XIV of France, claimed the throne, prompting an alliance of powers to prevent him succeeding. The danger was made greater by James's exile in France and his role in continual plots. With the army under the command of John Churchill, Duke of Marlborough, England joined the coalition opposing Philip. Marlborough had wielded considerable influence earlier in the reign, though for some years he had lived under the shadow of suspected Jacobite sympathies. The son of an impoverished Devon royalist, he had helped to quell the Monmouth Rebellion in 1685, but on William's landing he had joined him, being given an earldom to his earlier barony for his services. Part of his success was due to the close friendship of his wife, Sarah Churchill, with Princess Anne.

But to William should go much of the credit for Marlborough's victories during the war with France: his control of and interest in the army resulted in impressive reforms of men and materials, giving Marlborough subordinate officers of ability and, through war during the 1690s, experience.

William died from a hunting accident at Hampton Court, when his horse put a foot in a mole-hole and threw him, which incident gave rise to the Jacobite toast 'to the little gentleman in black velvet'. Despite only breaking a collarbone, his weakened body could not withstand the shock.

William III was: William I of Ireland; William II of Scotland; William III of England; William IV of Normandy.

Queen Anne and the Duke of Gloucester: studio of George Kneller, date unknown *(The National Portrait Gallery, London)*.

Anne

Born St James's Palace 1665. Ascended throne 1702. Reigned 12 years.
Second daughter of James II and Anne Hyde.
Married George, Prince of Denmark.
Two sons, three daughters (twelve others died soon after birth).
Died Kensington Palace 1714, aged 49 years. Buried at Westminster Abbey.

During the brief reign of James II, Anne had taken no part in politics; but on the landing of William of Orange she supported his accession to the throne. She was married to the dim but faithful Prince George of Denmark – of whom Charles II had commented unkindly if accurately: 'I have tried him drunk and tried him sober, and there is nothing in him.' An ordinary and at times vulgar woman, she had seventeen children, all of whom died, twelve of miscarriages, one was stillborn and five at an early age of hydrocephalus, better known as water on the brain.

Anne was thirty-seven years old when she succeeded, by which time her unrelenting pregnancies had so wrecked her health that she was a semi-invalid. She was closely bound to the Churchills, Lady Marlborough being a long-standing friend, and for most of her reign they exerted great influence over her and public affairs. Political strife between Whig and Tory rivals was keen, and was complicated by the question of who was to succeed Anne, an issue which was eventually to lead to a bitter quarrel with the Duke of Marlborough. Sarah Churchill lost her place as confidante due to her excessive demands and hectoring tone; it was taken by Abigail Hill, a cousin of the Duchess.

As Commander-in-Chief, Marlborough prosecuted the War of Spanish Succession with skill and vigour. His military genius dominated the scene: his popularity with the queen, his diplomacy and his victories, kept up the country's heart for war. For ten years he won every battle he fought and secured every town to which he laid siege, though the later stages of the war were difficult and some victories marginal.

The decisively won battles at Blenheim, Ramillies and Oudenarde gave England a position of influence in the world never previously attained. Peace came in 1713, with the signing of the Treaty of Utrecht, which laid the foundation of English colonial power in the eighteenth century. It also confirmed Louis's recognition of Anne's title, with the consequence that James Stuart, the Old Pretender, was ordered to leave France.

The queen, the last Stuart sovereign, was not in any way a clever woman; but the men surrounding her were exceptionally talented. This was a brilliant age: Swift and Pope, Addison and Steele were writing in verse and prose; Sir Christopher Wren was building St Paul's Cathedral; Locke and Newton were propounding new theories of philosophy and science.

The most important constitutional act of the reign was the sealing in 1707 of the Act of Union between England and Scotland, thereby forming Great Britain. It entailed the abolition of the Scottish Parliament in return for representation at Westminster and economic equality. The ecclesiastical settlement and laws in each country were not altered.

Anne was a staunch high-church Protestant. Her creation of 'Queen Anne's Bounty' for the increase of the incomes of the poorer clergy, restored to the Church a fund raised from tithes which Henry VIII had taken for his own use.

Principal Battles, 1485–1709

Bosworth Field   1485
Flodden   1513
Spurs   1513
Civil War Battles
    Edgehill   1642
    Worcester   1642 and 1651
    Devizes   1643
    Newbury   1643 and 1644
    Marston Moore   1644
    Naseby   1645
Sedgemoor   1685
Killiecrankie   1689

Boyne   1690
Spanish Succession
    Blenheim   1704
    Ramillies   1706
    Oudenarde   1708
    Malplaquet   1709

At Sea
    Cadiz   1576
    Spanish Armada   1588
    Beachy Head   1690

PART THREE

HANOVER

TO WINDSOR

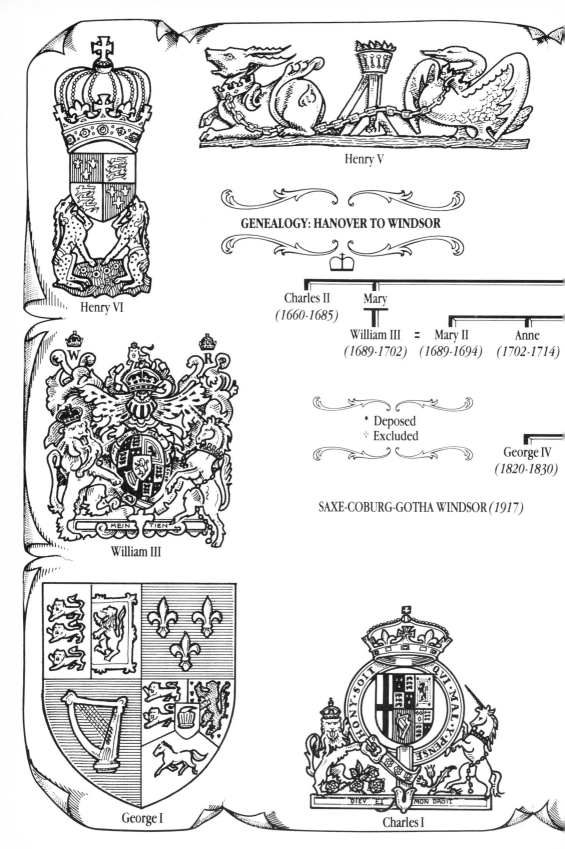

Henry V

GENEALOGY: HANOVER TO WINDSOR

Henry VI

| Charles II | Mary | | |
| (1660-1685) | | | |

William III = Mary II   Anne
(1689-1702) (1689-1694) (1702-1714)

* Deposed
÷ Excluded

George IV
(1820-1830)

SAXE-COBURG-GOTHA WINDSOR *(1917)*

William III

George I

Charles I

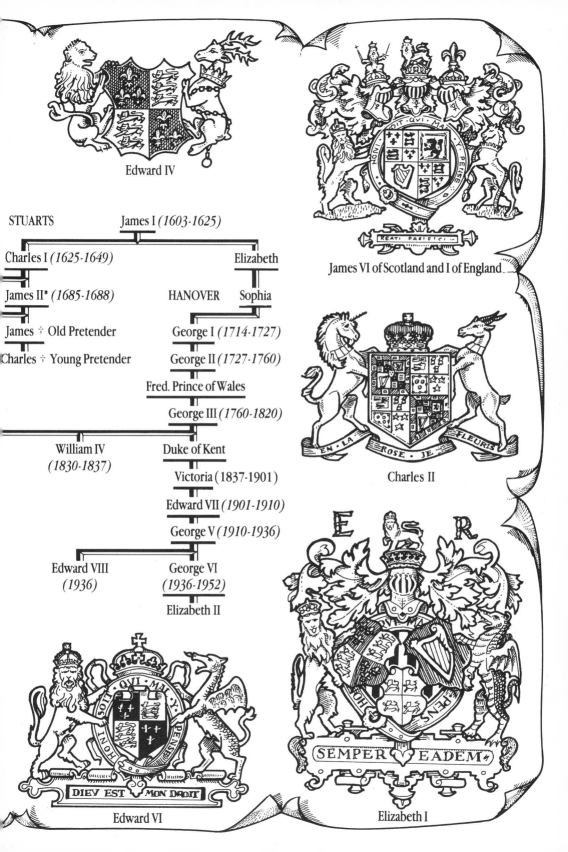

Edward IV

James VI of Scotland and I of England

Charles II

Elizabeth I

Edward VI

STUARTS   James I *(1603-1625)*

Charles I *(1625-1649)*   Elizabeth

James II* *(1685-1688)*   **HANOVER**   Sophia

James ÷ Old Pretender   George I *(1714-1727)*

Charles ÷ Young Pretender   George II *(1727-1760)*

Fred. Prince of Wales

George III *(1760-1820)*

William IV   Duke of Kent
(1830-1837)

Victoria *(1837-1901)*

Edward VII *(1901-1910)*

George V *(1910-1936)*

Edward VIII   George VI
(1936)   *(1936-1952)*

Elizabeth II

HANOVER TO WINDSOR

During the latter part of the seventeenth century, the question which dominated all others was that of the royal succession. In 1689, the deposed James II (1685–8) and his infant son James (b. 1688), were effectively excluded from the throne by Act of Parliament. The Act said that henceforth no Catholic, nor anyone married to a Catholic, could be sovereign of England.

William III (1689–1702) and his wife Mary II (died 1694) had no children. When the last of Queen Anne's seventeen children, the Duke of Gloucester, died in July 1700 at the age of ten, provision for the succession had to be made. The Act of Succession, 1701, vested it in the nearest Protestant relatives of the Stuarts – Sophia, the wife of the Elector of Hanover, and her descendants. Sophia was the fifth, and only Protestant, daughter of Elizabeth of Bohemia – James I's only daughter (see the family tree). This Act deliberately passed over the superior hereditary rights of the Stuarts, represented by the Catholic James II and his son; the Hanoverian claim was purely statutory – on the score of heredity the family had no real right to the throne. (In 1910 it was estimated that there were over 1,000 descendants of Charles I who had hereditary precedence over Queen Victoria, her son and grandson.)

Sophia of Hanover died two months before Queen Anne (1702–14), and on 1 August 1714 Sophia's son George Ludwig became the first Hanoverian king of England as George I. Hanover was an offshoot of the Duchy of Brunswick-Lüneberg, which had been governed by the Guelph family since the twelfth century; hence the Hanoverian kings were referred to in England as Hanoverians, as Guelphs or as the House of Brunswick.

The joint rulers of England and Hanover were:

George I   (1714–1727)
George II   (1727–1760)
George III   (1760–1820)
George IV   (1820–1830)
William IV   (1830–1837)

Opposite: George I: artist, Sir George Kneller, 1716 *(The National Portrait Gallery, London).*

103

The accession of Queen Victoria in 1837 saw the separation of England from Hanover, which had become a kingdom in 1815. As the succession to the throne of Hanover was governed by Salic law and therefore could not pass to a woman, it passed to the nearest male relative, Ernest, Duke of Cumberland, fifth son of George III; and to mark the change the German arms were removed from the royal arms of England, leaving them as they are today. Hanover was later swallowed up in Bismarck's Germany.

Edward VII, the eldest child of Queen Victoria and the Prince Consort, took his father's family name – that of Saxe-Coburg-Gotha – but popularly the royal family was still known as the House of Hanover or Brunswick. In July 1917, during World War I, King George V announced that he had abandoned all German titles for himself and his family, who would be known henceforth as the House of Windsor.

George I

Born Hanover 28 March 1660. Ascended throne 1714. Reigned 13 years.
Son of Ernest Augustus, Elector of Hanover.
Married Sophia Dorothea, Princess of Brunswick-Zell (1682).
One son, one daughter.
Died Osnabrück 11 June 1727, aged 67. Buried in Hanover.

Under the terms of the Act of Settlement, 1701, George Louis of Brunswick–Lüneberg, who had become Elector of Hanover in 1698, became king of England when Queen Anne died.

George I saw clearly that the Hanoverians had been brought in by the Whigs,* in preference to the Catholic Stuarts, merely as the lesser of two evils. Any line of action he initiated was likely to offend at least half the country. In fact George, aged fifty-four when he became king, had only a limited command of the English language and spent more time in Hanover than in England. His character was in any case ill-suited to the position.

The Court, always the centre of government, virtually ceased to exist except, at first, as a lively social forum. This was partly because George, with reason, mistrusted many of the noblemen around him; some had dabbled in treason and it was not surprising, therefore, that he preferred to rely on Hanoverians. George brought to England two mistresses but no wife: he had married his cousin Sophia in 1682, but dissolved the marriage in 1694. After George had taken a mistress following their marriage, Sophia had an affair with the Swedish Count Königsmarck; in 1694 the couple were surprised

---

*The terms Whig and Tory were both originally terms of contempt coined in the late seventeenth century. Whigs were Scottish 'whiggamores' or horse-drovers; Tories 'Irish robbers'.

and the Count killed. Sophia was confined to the castle of Ahlden where she died in 1726. The two children of the marriage were the future George II and Sophia Dorothea, who was to be the mother of Frederick the Great of Prussia.

Between George I and his son began the hostility between sovereign and heir-apparent which was to become traditional in the House of Hanover. It was reflected in the king's refusal to grant the Prince the status of Regent while the king returned to Hanover to attend to State matters. The Prince was denied any influence or responsibilities by his father, so it was readily assumed that while the king was away, the mice would play and intrigue against the king. Suspicion over the visits of the Secretary of State, Lord Townshend, to the Prince at Hampton Court while the king was away led to Townshend's dismissal. This kind of conflict was recurrent for much of the century.

Of George's mistresses, Horace Walpole left a vivid picture of Charlotte Sophia Kielmannsegge, later Countess of Darlington: 'I remember being terrified by her enormous figure . . . Two fierce black eyes, large and rolling beneath two lofty arched eyebrows, two acres of cheeks spread with crimson, an ocean of neck that overflowed and was not distinguished from the lower parts of her body, and no part restrained by stays – no wonder that a child dreaded such an ogress, and that the mob of London were highly diverted at the importation of so uncommon a seraglio!'

In common with other Hanoverians, George was rather stupid and as a lazy man only too content to leave the conduct of affairs in the hands of ministers, thereby transferring to their shoulders the responsibility for national policy. In choosing his ministers from among the Whigs, George laid the foundations of the Whig oligarchy which ruled England for the next fifty years. Cabinet government began in this reign, and Sir Robert Walpole (1676–1745), the chief minister of the majority party in the House of Commons, became England's first Prime Minister. His great chance came when the 'South Sea Bubble' burst in 1720: the South Sea Company, a highly speculative venture, had persuaded the government that it could redeem part of the national debt (see below); even the king was involved as investor and Governor of the Company. Walpole had strongly advised against it, and as First Lord of the Treasury he was able to salvage something from the wreakage that caused the death and loss of office of several ministers.

In 1715 the Jacobites, still supporting the Catholic Stuart line, attempted to supplant George I by James Edward Stuart, the 'Old Pretender', the son of James II. Led by the Earl of Mar, the rebels dispersed after the inconclusive Battle of Sheriffmuir, though another force reached Preston before surrendering. The rebellion failed miserably: the Pretender did not arrive in Britain for his one and only visit until it was over, and help promised by France never materialized because of the death of the French king, Louis XIV. A small Spanish force provided by Philip V landed in the Western Isles in 1719, but with little local support laid down its arms at Glenshiel.

One of George's first appointments was to restore Marlborough's command of the army. Though the Act of Settlement released Britain from any obligation to participate in hostilities involving George's Hanover, the use of an English fleet in the Baltic raised controversy. Part of the fear was a further increase in the national debt, which after the War of Spanish Succession stood at £54 million. The interest absorbed almost a third of all annual revenue. The country remained at peace until the prospect of an alliance of Spain and Austria created a diplomatic crisis, leading to war with Spain until 1726. After an abortive expedition against Spain's American possessions, Walpole, who had detested the necessary tax increase to pay for the war, negotiated the treaty of Seville in 1729.

By then, George was dead, having suffered a stroke at Osnabrück on 11 June 1727 while on his way to Hanover.

George II

Born Hanover 10 November 1683. Ascended throne 1727. Reigned 33 years.
Only son of George I.
Married Caroline of Ansbach-Bayreuth (1705).
Three sons, five daughters.
Died Kensington Palace 25 October 1760, aged 76. The last English king to be buried at Westminster Abbey.

George II, like his father before him, was first and foremost a German prince; but at least he knew English before he was too old to learn. Not much brighter than his father, George was short, unpredictable, impatient, meddlesome, courageous, a stickler for punctuality and routine, fond of music but none of the other arts. Importantly, he was capable of being bullied, and Queen Caroline of Ansbach was to exploit that fact in her support of Sir Robert Walpole whom George as Prince of Wales had disliked.

Unlike most Hanoverian kings, and despite a series of mistresses, George was devoted to his wife, who unfortunately died in 1737. There was, however, the usual Hanoverian friction between father and son, ending abruptly in 1751 with the death at Cliveden of Frederick, Prince of Wales. A contemporary wrote the epitaph:

Here lies poor Fred who was alive and is dead,
Had it been his father I had much rather,
Had it been his sister nobody would have missed her,
Had it been his brother, still better than another,
Had it been the whole generation, so much the better for the nation,
But since it is Fred who was alive and is dead,
There is no more to be said.

George II: artist, Thomas Hudson, 1744 *(The National Portrait Gallery, London)*.

George, like his father, had to rely on the Whigs, led at first by Walpole to whom the queen was a loyal and clever adviser. Walpole's methods and manners were crude, but his efficiency and desire for peace gave Britain a welcome respite and helped to establish the system of government through a Cabinet responsible to Parliament, which was in turn responsible to the electorate. Also, during the reigns of both George I and George II the Tories were suspect because of their associations with Jacobitism; as a consequence the custom was established that the Cabinet should consist of men of only one political party. This limited George's options for ministers, and no doubt contributed to his own sense of powerlessness.

Walpole's seeming impregnability led to a number of alliances against him, even amongst Whigs – it was then normal for a Whig or Tory ministry to have in opposition Members of the same allegiance. Walpole's opponents created an orgy of ministry-baiting, involving broadsheets, newspapers, ballads and libellous plays in the theatres. Walpole reacted badly to the insinuations. The opposition grew steadily, gradually eroding the regard in which he was held at Court. It was the extraordinary degree of ill-feeling between the Prince of Wales and his parents that heralded Walpole's fall. The king regarded his son as 'a monster and the greatest villain that ever was born'. The public felt much sympathy for the Prince's rejection, and his identification with the Opposition lifted their standing. The queen's death exacerbated Walpole's difficulties.

Against Walpole's wish, Britain drifted into war over the pragmatic sanction by which Maria Theresa had been guaranteed inheritance of her father's personal dominions. It was the beginning of a series of wars which was to last intermittently until 1815. In 1742 Walpole had to resign, dying three years later. The war extended, becoming the War of the Austrian Succession, aimed largely against France. Fighting began before war had been formally declared, and at Dettingen, in 1743, George II achieved the distinction of being the last reigning monarch to lead his subjects in the field. War against Spain followed an incident in which Captain Jenkins lost his ear, but which was more a pretext to challenge the Spanish monopoly of trade with South America than outrage at such treatment.

In 1745 the Jacobites tried once more to restore the Stuarts to the throne. Prince Charles Edward Stuart, the 'young Pretender', grandson of James II, landed at Eriskay in Scotland. At first he was much more successful than the protagonists of the 1715 uprising: Perth and Edinburgh were taken, Sir John Cope was defeated at Prestonpans, Carlisle fell and the Prince's army marched into Lancashire and on to Derby. But few rallied to his call, and a council of war in Derby determined on retreat. In April 1746 Charles was routed at Culloden Moor by the royal army under the king's second son, the Duke of Cumberland – 'Butcher Cumberland'.* Bonnie Prince Charlie escaped,

---

*The flower 'Sweet William' was named after him; in Scotland it is called 'Stinking Billie'.

lurking for six months in the Western Isles under the care of such loyal followers as Flora Macdonald; no one betrayed him, though a price of £30,000 was on his head. He moved later to France, dying a drunkard's death in Rome.

In 1756 the Seven Years War with France began, initially because of clashes in North America, though rivalries were also fierce in India where Clive's victory at Plassey (1757) paved the way for British rule. Wolfe's brilliant capture of Quebec by scaling the Heights of Abraham led to Canada becoming part of the British empire, and rich sugar islands like Martinique and Guadeloupe were taken. The British suffered severe reverses, and the government broke up. Against the king's wishes, William Pitt the Elder (1708–78), later Earl of Chatham, emerged as leader to meet the crisis.

George II died at Kensington on 25 October 1760, before the Seven Years War reached its successful conclusion.

The Change of Calendar, 1752

Juilius Ceasar in 46 BC fixed the length of the year at 365 days, and 366 days every fourth year. The months had thirty and thirty-one days alternately, with the exception of February (then the last month of the year), which had twenty-nine in ordinary years, and thirty in leap years. To mark this change of calendar July was named after its originator.

The Emperor Augustus upset this arrangement by naming August after himself, and in order that it should have the same number of days as July (thirty-one), took one day from February in both ordinary and leap years.

The *Julian* Calendar made a slight error in the length of the year, a mere eleven minutes and fourteen seconds; but by the sixteenth century the cumulative error was about ten days. This was rectified by Pope Gregory XIII who, in 1582, decreed that 5 October should become the fifteenth. In order to prevent a recurrence of the fault, it was ordained that the centurial years (1600, 1700, etc) should not be leap years unless divisible by 400.

England did not accept this *Gregorian* calendar until 1752, thereby causing much confusion between English and Continental dates, whilst the disparity between the Julian and Gregorian calendars was now eleven days. An Act of Parliament in 1750 made 3 September 1752 into 14 September and moved the first day of the year from 25 March (still reckoned as the beginning of the financial year) to 1 January. In this way England was brought into line with the rest of Europe. Russia did not adopt the Gregorian calendar until the Revolution of 1917.

George III

Born Norfolk House, St James's Square June 1738. Ascended throne 1760.
Reigned 59 years.
Son of Frederick Louis, Prince of Wales; Grandson of George II.
Married Charlotte of Mecklenburg-Strelitz (1761).
Nine sons, six daughters.
Died Windsor, 29 January 1820, aged 81. Buried at Windsor.

The first Hanoverian to be born in Britain, George was twenty-two when he ascended the throne, determined to rule as well as reign. He wished to recover the power of the Crown from the Prime Minister, and he temporarily succeeded in doing so. Parliament had no great popular support in the country, as too many MPs sat merely at the bidding of an individual patron. William Pitt, elected Prime Minister to meet a war crisis, which he did brilliantly, was unpopular afterwards with the Whigs in power.

During the first two decades of his reign, George worked methodically to break the power of the Whigs which had lasted since 1714. The Tories were able to shed their association with Jacobitism, now that the cause was well and truly dead. George was also determined to bring his tutor, Lord Bute, into the administration, which raised the thorny issue of the king's right to appoint ministers. In keeping with customary political methods, he used bribery to create his own party, the 'King's friends', and changed the composition of his ministries with extraordinary frequency and little obvious sense of purpose. Lord Bute, with little experience of government, could not stand the heat and, to George's disappointment, quit after less than a year. The king finally made a wise choice with the appointment of Lord North as first minister.

On his accession, George wanted an immediate end to the war with France, but before peace was negotiated, Britain was also at war with France's new ally, Spain. The Treaty of Paris (1763) confirmed Britain's position as the leading colonial power.

George III and Lord North must bear the responsibility for the loss of England's North American colonies. The colonists were exasperated by repeated attempts by the British government to impose taxes on them. Higher taxes were needed to pay for the mounting costs of military and naval forces protecting the colonists and to offset the huge loss in tax revenues caused by smuggling; an estimate of 1763 suggested that only one-tenth of imported tea was subjected to the statutory duty. The colonists' anger found outlets in incidents like the 'Boston Tea Party' (1773), and in 1775 war finally broke out.

The colonists unrealistically tried to use the king as an intermediary, petitioning him for protection against his ministers. The king's role became more active, hiring five battalions of troops in Hanover and supporting North. When France and Spain came

George III: studio of A. Ramsay, c.1767 *(The National Portrait Gallery, London)*.

into the war on the side of the colonists, and the Opposition clamoured for peace, the outcome was inevitable. The colonists proclaimed their independence on 4 July 1776, and achieved it at the Peace of Versailles signed in 1783. George's obstinacy in dealing with people whom he believed to be rebels had much to do with the causes of the war and its needless protraction. The Whigs in general had no clear ideas on colonial policy; they still thought of colonies merely as markets for British goods. But they soon saw that the recovery of the American colonies was impossible, particularly after the British surrender at Yorktown, and refused to support the king in continuing the war.

This brought to an end George III's period of personal rule. In 1783 he resigned much ministerial power to the twenty-four-year-old William Pitt the Younger (1759–1806), famous son of a famous father; a Tory, he was to be Prime Minister with only one break (1801–4) until his death in 1806.

George III had married Charlotte of Mecklenburg-Strelitz, who was brought over to England by a squadron of yachts under the command of Lord Anson, the Admiral who captained the second circumnavigation of the globe by an English ship. George was devoted to her, and at first to their fifteen children (nine sons and six daughters), but the tradition of hostility between reigning monarch and the heir-apparent later developed strongly. However, George broke the family tradition in being a model of domestic virtues, eschewing the open womanizing of his ancestors.

The king was highly neurotic with a flair for music, furniture and gardens; he liked making buttons and putting watches together (his grandfather had enjoyed an eccentric passion for cutting out paper figures). He was keenly interested in the agricultural improvements which took place during his reign; the creation of model farms on his estate at Windsor earned him the nickname of 'Farmer George'. He was a patron of the sciences and the arts, and his collection of books laid the foundation for the future British Museum Library.

During the closing years of his reign, he had little influence on English affairs. His mind had always been weak and vindictive, and after 1811 he was at times both blind and insane, exacerbated by the critical illness of his favourite child, Princess Amelia. His violent outbursts had to be restrained by the use of a straitjacket. His eldest son, George, ruled for him as Prince Regent.

England was guided through the long French Revolutionary and Napoleonic Wars (1793–1815) by Pitt and the military and naval genius of such men as the Duke of Wellington (1769–1852) and Lord Nelson (1758–1805).

Significant changes were made under George in Ireland: violence extracted the concessions of legislative independence in 1782 and the Catholic vote in 1793, but Pitt the Elder fell over the issue of full emancipation, which George refused. None the less the Act of Union in 1801 joined the two countries until home rule was established in 1920–1. Catholic emancipation was finally granted under George IV in 1829.

Other radical reforms included the introduction of income tax by Pitt in 1799, intended to be temporary and to help to finance the war against France. In 1807 the slave trade was abolished in lands under British control, but slavery continued in British possessions until 1833.

Besides great statesmen like Pitt and Fox, and great captains like Wellington and Nelson, George III's long reign was graced by some of the greatest names in English literature: Johnson, Gibbon, Cowper, Crabbe, Scott, Jane Austen, Byron, Coleridge, Wordsworth, Southey, Shelley and Keats. Artists like Reynolds (the first President of the Royal Academy, founded in 1768), Gainsborough and Romney founded a school of English painters.

The pace of change in England during the eighteenth century accelerated as the century neared its close. The population more than doubled, stimulating far-reaching changes in agriculture and industry in order to keep pace with the growing demands for food and manufactured goods. During George III's reign, despite the growth in output, higher tax revenues and a fourfold increase in foreign trade, the national debt rose from £138 million to £800 million, largely as a result of costly wars. Transport was revolutionized, with new roads, tramways and the first canals. (George, however, took little advantage of the new turnpike roads, never venturing further than an annual holiday in Weymouth during the 1790s.)

George III died on 29 January 1820, having spent the last nine years of his reign in seclusion. He was succeeded by his eldest son George, the Prince Regent, as George IV.

The American War of Independence, 1775–83

The train of events that was to lead to the independence of the American colonies began with the Seven Years War and the difficult task of dislodging the French from their chain of redoubts stretching from Pennsylvania, along the Ohio River and down to the Mississippi. The French had intended them to mark the boundaries of their 'interior' empire west of the Appalachians. With some Indian tribes as allies, the French succeeded in fending off, first the Virginians, and later much larger numbers of troops sent from Britain and the colonies, even when heavily outnumbered. Six years' fighting were required to win control of Canada and the French lands beyond the Appalachians.

The question for the British government was how to organize this huge area. Clearly the lax control of previous years had to be replaced by something more formal – and costly – as was the case in India after the Mutiny. It was the ham-fisted way in which unimaginative and ill-informed ministers in London tried to resolve this problem, combined with the experience of colonists fighting together against the French, that created a unity amongst states that had previously had little common ground but language. This unity was forged by the colonists' response to a series of measures

The American War of Independence 1775–82: Signing the Declaration of Independence: engraved after Trumbull *(Hulton–Deutsch Collection)*

designed by the British government to raise money to pay for the defence and administration of the colonies.

Laws restricting American trade and increasing export taxes on European goods sold to America inevitably irritated the colonists, as did the declaration that all land west of the Appalachians was Crown property closed to settlers. But it was not until the Stamp Act of 1765 that feelings boiled over; those responsible for selling the stamps which were to be affixed to just about everything had a rough time, and within a year the Act was repealed. Jubilation soon ended when George III and his compliant minister Lord North imposed a further catalogue of taxes and restrictions, the most infamous being that on tea. Precisely who started what at Boston in 1770 no one can say, but a fight outside the Customs House caused the death of five people. From the protest meetings sprang articulate argument and propaganda against what were seen as unwarrantable interferences with the Colonists' freedoms. The celebrated Boston Tea Party (1773) is only the best known of the acts of sabotage directed against North's taxes.

The knee-jerk response of the British government was to send troops to impose order, as well as closing the port of Boston to all trade. From here on, the movement amongst colonists appears in retrospect to have developed a momentum of its own. Groups sprang up to express grievances, and the Virginians led the way in the treasonable act of setting up a Provincial Convention, an independent legislature. The

Declaration of Independence (1776), largely written by Thomas Jefferson, was agreed on all but two points by a vote of twelve of the colonies/states, and formed the manifesto of the justices for which the colonists were prepared to fight. With the expectation of help from France and Spain, the colonists took up arms. The first clash, at Concord, Massachusetts, went to the colonists and inspired others. The superiority of the colonists' rifled barrels over the British smooth-bore muskets for the kind of scrappy engagements that characterized much of the war, was a significant factor in helping untrained colonists from all walks of life to defeat a professional army.

With George Washington in command of the colonists' forces, the war at first went badly for them: Philadelphia was lost and the first winter saw Washington's troops decimated by illness, only saved by the timely arrival of French *matériel* and soldiers. Washington's dogged determination won the war, creating a legend barely diminished by his peacetime shortcomings.

George III and many in Britain were dumbfounded that the American colonies could have been lost. But in defeat he displayed a regal magnanimity; he greeted America's first Minister to the Court of St James's, John Adams, with the gallant words: 'I will be very frank with you. I was the last to consent to the separation: but the separation having been made, and having become inevitable, I have always said, as I say now, that I would be the first to meet the friendship of the United States as an independent power.'

French Revolutionary and Napoleonic Wars, 1793–1815

In 1793 England and a coalition of other European powers went to war against the French revolutionaries who, having seized power and overthrown the monarchy in France, seemed bent on conquering Europe. The invasion by France of the Austrian Netherlands, with its threat to Britain's maritime interests, was the deciding factor. France's declaration of war in 1793, much to George's delight, was followed by an ignominious campaign in Flanders under the Duke of York that ended in a retreat through Germany and evacuation in 1795. However, the Duke's reforms of the corruption and barbaric conditions in the army were vital for Britain's ability to withstand the French onslaught.

But at sea the war began more auspiciously: conquests of French territories were made in the West Indies, followed by the capture of Corsica, Pondicherry, Trincomalee and Ceylon. A French invasion of Ireland in 1796 was only aborted due to bad weather, and plans to invade England frustrated by naval victories that helped to make 1797 the turning point of the war, despite the fact that Britain now stood alone. Nelson and Jervis inflicted substantial damage on the Spanish fleet at Cape St Vincent (William, Duke of

Clarence, later William IV, fought in this battle). At Camperdown Duncan won a decisive engagement against the Dutch fleet that eliminated its ability to act as a spearhead for the invasion of England. Britain's naval supremacy was consolidated by Nelson's total victories at Aboukir Bay (1798), which nullified Napoleon's gains on land in Egypt, and at Copenhagen (1801). In 1798 the second coalition of Britain, Russia, Turkey, Naples, Portugal and Austria was formed, but fell apart in 1801. Peace was made at Amiens in 1802.

Napoleon Bonaparte (1769–1821) who seized supreme power in France in 1801 and who was to become Emperor in 1804, used the next few months to reorganize the French fighting forces prior to launching an attack against England. War was renewed in 1803. For two years Napoleon tried to invade England, but his schemes were hampered by a third coalition between Britain, Russia, Austria, Sweden and Naples and ruined by Nelson's defeat of the combined French and Spanish fleets off Cape Trafalgar in 1805. However, in Europe Napoleon won a series of victories against the Austrians, Russians and Prussians.

Napoleon then resorted to economic warfare in an attempt to bankrupt the 'nation of shopkeepers' by the Continental System, excluding British trade from European countries or colonies, but Britain's navy frustrated his plans. Moreover, the subject nations grew increasingly tired of French tyranny. Napoleon's use of Spain, both as part of the Continental System and to help partition Portugal, backfired when the Spanish people rose up in May 1808 and, after slaughtering any Frenchmen they could find, appealed to Britain for help. With the landing of British forces under Arthur Wellesley, later Duke of Wellington, and the ensuing Peninsular War (1808–13), British troops were to remain on the Continent until after Waterloo.

With Napoleon's invasion of Russia in 1812, it became evident that Napoleon had overreached himself: he had had to commit 30,000 troops to hold the Iberian peninsula, and was compelled to withdraw many for his disastrous campaign in Russia, allowing Wellesley to drive the French forces back into France by the end of 1813. At Leipzig (1813) the combined armies of the fourth coalition decisively defeated the French. The English blockade of Europe at this time caused much trouble with neutral countries, and the Anglo-American War, which broke out in 1812, lasted until 1814.

Peace negotiations with the French were opened in 1814. Napoleon was exiled to Elba from where he escaped, returned to France, and began his 'Hundred Days Campaign' which ended with 25,000 French dead on the field of Waterloo in 1815. Napoleon was exiled to St Helena, where he died in 1821.

George IV

Born St James's Palace 12 August 1762. Ascended throne 1820.
Reigned 9 years.
Eldest son of George III.
Married (i) Mrs Maria Fitzherbert (1785); (ii) Caroline of Brunswick-Wolfenbuttell
(1795)
One daughter.
Died Windsor 26 June 1830, aged 67 years. Buried at Windsor.

'He will be either the most polished gentleman, or the most accomplished blackguard in Europe – possibly both', said the tutor of the future George IV when he was fifteen.

From Carlton House, where he set up his own establishment in 1783, 'the first gentleman of Europe' became the leader of fashionable London society, setting the pattern in dress and patronizing the arts and architecture. He 'discovered' Brighton and had the Pavilion built in 1784. Regent Street and Regent's Park were laid out and named after him for the encouragement he gave to the architect John Nash; the term 'Regency style' passed into the English language. No monarch has done more for the artistic and architectural wealth of the country.

Both before and during his reign, George IV did much harm to the cause of monarchy. Subjects who had grown accustomed to the irreproachable family affairs of George III were exasperated by his immorality. His reckless extravagance was the more conspicuous at a time when the after-effects of the Napoleonic Wars and the upheaval of the Industrial Revolution were causing much social distress and misery. As a result he was probably the most despised of all monarchs, the subject of astonishingly vicious attacks by caricaturists and columnists. As Prince of Wales, his coach was hissed and pelted in the streets of London. He was a great embarrassment to Lord Liverpool's government which, though committed to *laissez-faire* economics and far from reform-minded, was concerned to reduce costs and ease poverty.

George had a steady flow of mistresses while he was Prince Regent; this was stemmed in 1785 when he married secretly a twice-married young Catholic widow, Mrs Maria Fitzherbert. Since he married without the king's consent, the union was invalid under the Royal Marriage Act of 1772; in any case a prince married to a Catholic would not be allowed to succeed to the throne. The Prince of Wales was dishonest enough to later deny that any marriage to Mrs Fitzherbert had taken place.

So in 1795, in order to placate his father who refused to settle his debts on any other terms, George married his cousin, Caroline of Brunswick. He treated her abominably throughout their married life together, which barely survived the birth of their only child early in 1796. Between 1814 and 1820 she lived with an Italian abroad, but to

George IV: artist Thomas Lawrence, date unknown *(The National Portrait Gallery, London)*.

George's annoyance returned when he became king to assert her place as queen. Her popularity amongst the populace was in marked contrast to feelings about George, and his attempts to divorce Caroline disgusted the country.

From 1811, as Prince Regent, he was king in all but name. The death of George III in 1820 gave him the title of king without altering in any way the situation which had existed since 1811. George IV's first act at his accession was to attempt to exclude his wife's name from the traditional prayers offered for the royal family; and he succeeded in having her excluded from his coronation in July 1821.

That George while Prince of Wales had befriended the Whigs to annoy his father rather from conviction, was borne out by his continuing his father's appointment of Tory ministers. His reign saw a further contraction of the monarch's powers, due to the straitened financial position of the monarch, the growing complexity of government and the reduction of perquisites, pensions and places with which monarchs had been accustomed to buy support and power. George failed in his attempts to oppose some of the major changes of his reign, such as Catholic emancipation (1829) or the recognition of the newly independent South American republics. The difficulty of governments working with George IV, particularly when he was in a tantrum or prone to incoherent and interminable arguments, convinced the Whigs that when power was theirs, they would impose Charles James Fox's dictum that a monarch should reign but not rule.

This coincided with popular demands for Parliamentary reform, which was seen as the key to improving the lot of the working- and middle-classes. During George's Regency, there were many demonstrations in favour of reform, and many thought the country on the verge of revolution. Mass meetings often ended in violence, most notably in Manchester where the Peterloo massacre (1819) left eleven dead, but dragoons were to be seen on the streets of many towns, particularly in the north. Troops had to be used, since the metropolitan police force was not established by Sir Robert Peel until 1829, and throughout the rest of the country until the middle of the century. In 1820 a plot to assassinate the cabinet was discovered and the protagonists arrested in a hayloft at Marylebone; the five ringleaders were hung. The government response was suppression, and the Six Acts of 1819 were designed to prohibit public meetings and curb the radical press.

But George IV was not without either intelligence or aptitudes: his faults were the result of indolence and lack of application. He had a sensitive appreciation of literature; he was a fervent admirer of Jane Austen and kept a set of her novels in each of his residences. 'I shall always reflect with pleasure', he said, 'on Sir Walter Scott's having been the first creation of my reign.' When George visited Scotland in 1822, Scott organised a magnificent reception for him. George gave his father's library to form the basis of the British Museum Library, and persuaded the government to buy the

Angerstein collection of pictures which formed the basis of the National Gallery. George was, in addition, probably the wittiest of all monarchs, Charles II excepted.

After his father's reclusiveness, he revived royal travels, journeying to Hanover, Scotland and Ireland, where he was the first visiting monarch since Richard II. Having a sense of theatre, George was well suited to public appearances, which did something to diminish the hostility his Regency had aroused. 'He was the most extraordinary compound of talent, wit, buffoonery, obstinacy and good feelings, in short, a medley of the most opposite qualities, with a great preponderance of good – that I ever saw in any character in my life,' was the Duke of Wellington's summation of him.

His earlier energy sapped by corpulence, George IV died on 26 June 1830, an event hailed with relief. The report in *The Times* reveals, besides its low opinion of the man, how outspoken the press of the day was about the monarchy:

> There never was an individual less regretted by his fellow creatures than this deceased king . . . What eye has wept for him? What heart has heaved one throb of unmercenary sorrow . . . for that Leviathan of the *haut ton* George IV . . . Nothing more remains to be said about George IV but to pay, as we must, for his profusion; and to turn his bad conduct to some account by tying up the hands of those who come after him in what concerns the public money.

George IV was succeeded by his brother, the Duke of Clarence, as William IV, because his only legitimate child, Princess Charlotte, had died in 1817.

William IV

Born Buckingham Palace 21 August 1765. Ascended throne 1830.
Reigned 6 years.
Third son of George III.
Married Adelaide of Saxe-Coburg and Meiningen (1818).
Two daughters.
Died Windsor 20 June 1837, aged 71. Buried at Windsor.

Following the death in childbirth of Princess Charlotte in 1817, William, Duke of Clarence, and his brothers, the Dukes of York, Kent and Cambridge, were prevailed upon to quit their middle-aged semi-retirement in order to secure the succession. When the elder brother, the Duke of York,* died in 1827, William became heir to the throne.

*The 'Noble Duke of York' of the nursery rhyme, Commander-in-Chief of the British Army between 1798 and 1827. He was no military general but a very able administrator.

Known as the 'sailor king', William IV had entered the navy in 1779 at the age of thirteen and saw service in America and the West Indies, becoming an Admiral of the Fleet in 1811 and a violent and difficult Lord High Admiral for a year from 1827. On his accession, William was popular: his unassuming character, exemplary private life (at least since his marriage – from 1790 to 1811 he had lived at Bushey Park with the actress Mrs Jordan, by whom he had had ten children) and his known hatred of pomp and ceremonial (he even wanted to dispense with the coronation) rendered him an agreeable contrast to George IV. William had lived in relative poverty, the press speculating who kept who at Bushey Park (Mrs Jordan continued her career in the theatre).

The great question in 1830 was Parliamentary reform. George IV had been resolutely opposed to any and every reform. In 1830 Wellington's Tory administration lost the general election despite the king's support, the first time this had happened. Lord Grey won on a ticket of Parliamentary reform, to which William was inevitably opposed, meaning as it would a further decline in the monarch's power. After a difficult passage a reform bill was piloted through the lower chamber in 1831, but its continual rejection by the Lords brought England close to revolution again. The new, articulate middle-class insisted that no longer could the hereditary landowners remain solely responsible for a nation so urgently needing financial, economic and social overhaul. William refused to create the peers demanded by the Whigs to enable the bill to pass through the Lords. Grey resigned, but when the Tories proved unable to form an administration, William relented and though still against the reform conceded that 'as a sovereign it was his duty to put those feelings and prejudices aside'. To such *realpolitik,* William probably owed his throne, for during a period of revolutions that threw other European countries into turmoil, he was the only European monarch of his day to survive the advent of democracy.

The Reform Act was passed in 1832. It extended the franchise to the middle-class on the basis of property qualifications; it left the working-classes bitterly disappointed, and encouraged the development of the Chartist movement to persuade the government to introduce universal male suffrage* and effect other reforms that are now taken for granted, such as voting by ballot and payment of MPs. None the less the Reform Act did mean that the landowning class had at last decided to share government with the more prosperous tenant farmers, skilled artisans and industrialists. As for the monarchy, the history of the Reform Bill's passage meant that yet another weapon in the monarch's arsenal had been appropriated by party politics – the control of peerages. It also marked a new ascendancy of Commons over Lords.

---

*Subsequent Acts of 1867, 1884, 1918, 1928 and 1969 gradually extended the franchise, until by 1969 all men and women over the age of eighteen had a vote.

Above: William IV: artist M. A. Shee, date unknown *(The National Portrait Gallery, London).*
Opposite: Queen Victoria: artist, Sir George Hayter 1863, after a portrait of 1838 *(The National Portrait Gallery, London).*

A few months after William's accession, the Liverpool & Manchester Railway was opened to great acclaim. The forerunner of the modern railway, it was the world's first public railway to be entirely operated by steam locomotives from the outset over its own tracks. Its success in lowering prices of raw materials, finished goods and food, because of the huge savings railways offered in transport costs, brought about the railway age. The adoption of Greenwich time (or Railway time) as standard throughout the country was only made possible by the railway, reflecting the way that accelerated journeys helped to impose a uniformity of products, ideas and manners over the country. Queen Victoria was the first monarch to travel by train.

In 1833 slavery was abolished in British colonies, thereby completing the work begun in 1807; the government set aside £20 million as compensation for the slave owners. The Poor Law was reformed in 1834, for the first time since 1601 – although this measure created the workhouse system, so graphically depicted by Dickens in the pages of *Oliver Twist*. In 1834 the Houses of Parliament burned down, to be replaced by the present buildings, which were designed by Barry and Pugin. Local government was reformed in 1835.

When William died on 20 June 1837, the press was no more complimentary or less forthright than for George IV: the *Spectator* commented that 'though at times jovial and, for a king, an honest man, [William] was a weak, ignorant, commonplace sort of person . . . Notwithstanding his feebleness of purpose and littleness of mind, his ignorance and his prejudices, William IV was to the last a popular sovereign, but his very popularity was acquired at the price of something like public contempt.'

Victoria

Born Kensington Palace 24 May 1819. Ascended throne 1837. Reigned 63 years.
Daughter of Edward, Duke of Kent, and Victoria Maria Louisa of Saxe-Coburg;
granddaughter of George III.
Married Prince Albert of Saxe-Coburg (1840).
Four sons, five daughters.
Died Osborne 22 January 1901, aged 81. Buried Frogmore, Windsor. *

> I sing of Georges four.
> Since Providence could stand no more
> Some say that far the worst
> Of all was George the First.
> But yet by some 'tis reckoned
> That worse still was George the Second.
> And what mortal ever heard,
> Any good of George the Third?
> When George the Fourth from the earth descended,
> Thank God the line of Georges ended.
>
> (Walter Savage Landor, 1775–1864)

Landor's bitter lines give some indication of eighteen-year-old Queen Victoria's heritage in 1837. William IV had been a great improvement on his brother, but he was not an impressive figure. The throne which Queen Victoria inherited was weak and unpopular and it took her a long time to live down the irreverence with which the nation had treated her Hanoverian uncles.

Victoria's coronation was something of a fiasco, with a Lord rolling down the steps of the Abbey, the altar at St Edward's Chapel being covered with plates of sandwiches and bottles of wine, and the Archbishop putting the ring on the wrong finger. There was some question of a Regency, despite her age, on account of her inexperience, but this was part of a typically disagreeable intrigue by Sir John Conroy to paint Victoria incapable of assuming the responsibilities of a queen in the hope that he would be appointed Regent. It was soon realized that Victoria was perfectly capable of performing her duties.

Victoria was the only child of the second marriage of Princess Victoria of Saxe-Coburg to Edward, Duke of Kent, fourth son of George III. Her father died when she was eight months old, and his place was filled by her uncle Leopold of Saxe-Coburg (later King of the Belgians). He was responsible for the general character of her early

---

*The queen did not wish to be buried amongst her Hanoverian uncles.

education, and remained a faithful correspondent. Victoria had a sheltered childhood, seldom mixing with girls her own age, which made for the maturity and firmness she displayed in the early years of her reign. Despite spending her childhood largely at Kensington Palace (then less a part of London than now), she saw little of the royal family due to William's dislike of the Duchess of Kent. He was barely able to conceal his feelings about her, and was furious over her royal progresses round the Isle of Wight with her daughter when, under the prompting of the unpleasant Sir John Conroy, she exacted royal salutes from the king's batteries and ships. 'The popping must stop,' ordered the king.

An early example of her independence was her refusal to change her ladies-in-waiting after the fall of Melbourne's government. Many of the ladies-in-waiting were related to Whig ministers and it had been the custom to change them when a new administration came to power. For this expression of personal will, the London mob shouted 'Mrs Melbourne' after her during what was called the 'Bedchamber crisis', another indication of public disrespect for the monarchy at the beginning of her reign.

In February 1840 the Saxe-Coburg influence upon her life was strengthened by her marriage to her cousin, Albert of Saxe-Coburg-Gotha (1819–61). Tactless, serious, intelligent, conscientious and very German, Albert never endeared himself to the English people. There was no precedent, maintained the Archbishop of Canterbury, for his being included in the customary prayers for the royal family; he was excluded from any official position in the political life of the country; although he was made a British citizen, he was never granted the titular dignity of an English peer; nor, until he and Queen Victoria had been married for seventeen years (1857), was he made Prince Consort. Prince Albert, however, did quietly exert tremendous influence over the queen, a fact which became fully apparent only after his death.

He proved to be a devoted husband and father, and helped to raise the monarchy to the lofty pinnacle of respectability where it has since remained. He left two permanent legacies to England: one was the Christmas tree, which he introduced from his native Germany; the other grew out of the Crystal Palace Exhibition of 1851, behind which Albert was the driving force. Six million people visited the Exhibition, which showed a profit of £186,000. With the money, thirty acres of land were purchased in Kensington, to be developed as a shrine to science and art. This land now bears, amongst similar institutions, the Victoria and Albert Museum, the Science Museum, the Imperial College of Science and Technology, the Royal College of Music and the Royal Albert Hall.

The death of the Prince Consort from typhoid on 14 December 1861 was followed by the queen's withdrawal to the seclusion of Osborne, Balmoral, Windsor or the Riviera, for a period of mourning which, despite mounting public criticism, lasted until the Golden Jubilee celebrations in 1887. It allowed people to ask what value the country was deriving from the monarchy, fuelling republican sentiments. Parliament expressed

Queen Victoria opening The Great Exhibition of 1851 *(Hulton–Deutsch Collection)*.

its displeasure by growing reluctance to grant money for the civil list. Fortunately for Victoria, imperial developments distracted the country's attention.

During her seclusion the queen was not inactive. Her husband had taught her to be a conscientious public servant, and she gave close attention to daily routine business and administration, at a time when great political and social reforms were transforming Britain. None the less her continual absence from the seat of government meant that much of her work was a formality and entailed little exercise of real power, except in the choice of ministers. As late as 1892 she put her foot down over having Henry Labouchere in the Cabinet unless he gave up the radical paper *Truth* which he had founded, and in 1895 stopped Henry Mathews' reappointment as Home Secretary. The only legislation that can be ascribed to Victoria was the Public Worship Bill of 1874, doing away with Popish trappings from the Anglican Church.

The chief advances through legislation were the Mines Act (1842) forbidding the employment of women and children underground; the repeal of the Corn Laws in 1846; various factory acts which eventually established a ten-hour day; several Public Health acts from 1848; the Education Act of 1870, which introduced universal elementary education in England and Wales; the Artisans' Dwelling Act (1875); Trades Union Acts (1871 and 1876) and the Reform Acts of 1867 and 1884 which widened the franchise. A measure of the way society was transformed during Victoria's reign and took on many of the elements of today's world is that in 1868, for example, flogging in the army during peacetime and the transportation of criminals were abolished, and the Trades Union Congress was formed.

These Acts were implemented by the ten Prime Ministers of Victoria's reign: Lord Melbourne, Sir Robert Peel, Lord John Russell, Lord Derby, Lord Aberdeen, Viscount Palmerston, Benjamin Disraeli, William Ewart Gladstone, Lord Rosebery and Lord Salisbury. Melbourne and Disraeli had the greatest influence over the queen, Melbourne acting as her colourful tutor on English history, a subject inevitably seldom touched upon by her Uncle Leopold. Victoria was particularly well disposed towards Disraeli; after his death in 1881, the queen returned to Disraeli's house, Hughenden Manor in Buckinghamshire, which she had visited in 1877, just so that she could sit in his study and recall the man whose career she regarded as 'one of the most remarkable in the annals of the Empire'. She would never have written anything complimentary about Gladstone whom she disliked intensely; she once complained that he addressed her as if she were a public meeting. It was to Gladstone that she sent perhaps her most stinging telegram; she was staying at Holker Hall when Khartoum fell and General Gordon was killed, whereupon she cabled the Prime Minister: 'To think that all this might have been prevented and many precious lives saved by earlier action is too frightful.' Its truth did not help Gladstone to forgive the rebuke.

During Victoria's reign the British Empire doubled in size, principally with additions in Africa and India. New Zealand became a part in 1840. The status of some older colonies changed: Canada became a Dominion in 1867 and the six colonies of Australia made into a Commonwealth in 1900. The Empire was consolidated and expanded, though with much more difficulty, in Burma, the Pacific, Egypt, southern Africa and India. Wars were fought in Afghanistan, Zululand, Egypt, the Sudan and South Africa (Boer Wars in 1881 and 1899–1902), and a mutiny suppressed in India (1857), before English rule was finally established in those countries. In India the change was fundamental: the Mutiny made inevitable the full assumption of formal sovereignty over British India, taking over many of the former responsibilities of the East India Company.

Victoria took particular pleasure from her title of Queen-Empress of India, bestowed upon her by Disraeli in 1876. (She even acquired an Indian servant after the 1877 Jubilee celebrations when Indian princes and a cavalry escort were present to pay their respects.) In 1875 Disraeli purchased the controlling interest in the Suez Canal. Apart from participation in the Crimean War (1853–6), during which the queen introduced the Victoria Cross, England was involved in no major European entanglements between 1815 and 1914.

The queen's unique position at the head of one large European family was probably a contributory factor in keeping her country at peace. She was related, either directly or by marriage, to the royal houses of Germany, Russia, Greece, Romania, Sweden,

Queen Victoria wearing the small Imperial Crown and photographed for her 66th birthday in 1855 *(The Mansell Collection)*.

Denmark, Norway and Belgium. The Tsar of All the Russias was her 'dear Nicky', and the Emperor of Germany, the dreaded Kaiser Wilhelm II, was 'Willy' her own grandson. Queen Victoria ruled her own, and this wider European family, despotically.

The queen's tastes, her virtues and her limitations, reflected those of the middle-class generally. She disliked all 'modern' music ('You couldn't drink a cup of tea to that,' she remarked of a drinking-song by Rubenstein); she found 'modern' paintings odd. Perhaps partly due to the strong sense of duty imbibed from Prince Albert, Victoria had little time for 'the society of fashionable and fast people', as she phrased it, the very people whose company Edward, Prince of Wales relished. The obverse of this distaste for the indulgent and dissolute preoccupations of some of the aristocracy was a rejection of class divisions and a warm regard for the lower orders. Her friendship with the forthright John Brown was, for many, an uncomfortable expression of her preferences. On women's suffrage and extensions of the democratic process, however, Victoria had a reactionary view, though she thought of herself as a liberal. Until Victoria's reign few people would have had any accurate visual knowledge of the royal family; the invention of photography and the millions of *cartes-de-visite* sold of her portrait changed that.

The advent of railways enabled Victoria to travel as no monarch before her. At first Victoria and Albert used the Royal Pavilion at Brighton as an escape from London, but the insatiable curiosity of the people meant that they were mobbed on arrival at Brighton station. A remote house was wanted and found in 1845 at Osborne on the Isle of Wight, the Italianate house becoming their principal country refuge in England. For longer periods away from the capital, the purchase of Balmoral in 1842 provided a Scottish baronial retreat. Victoria developed a particular attachment to the Highlands, which offered her the peace and solitude her retiring nature craved. Even Balmoral was too busy, and she spent much of her time on the estate at the small villa she built in the late 1860s beside Loch Muick. After the death of Albert, Buckingham Palace was hardly used for forty years (Edward referred to it as 'the Sepulchre'), Victoria preferring to stay at Windsor. Victoria was the first British sovereign to visit France officially (1855) since the coronation in Paris of Henry VI in 1431.

Queen Victoria died in the sixty-fourth year of her reign* on 22 January 1901; it was not just the end of a reign but the end of an era. She had reigned three years longer, and was three days older at the time of her death, than George III. During that time France had known two dynasties and become a republic; Spain had seen three monarchs and Italy four. She was succeeded by her eldest son as Edward VII.

---

*Longest reigns: Louis XIV of France, born 1638, reigned for seventy-two years, 1643–1715; Francis Joseph, Austrian Emperor, born 1830, died in 1916 after a reign of sixty-eight years, 1848–1916.

Queen Victoria with John Brown: photographed by Wilson, Whitlock and Downey, date unknown *(The National Portrait Gallery, London)*.

Queen Victoria was survived by six children, forty grandchildren and thirty-seven great-grandchildren – including four future sovereigns: Edward VII, George V, Edward VIII and George VI.

The Family of Queen Victoria and the Prince Consort
1 Princess Victoria (1840–1901) married Frederick, later Crown Prince of Prussia and Frederick III. Their son became Wilhelm II. A daughter married the King of Greece.
2 Edward VII (1841–1910) married the daughter of the King of Denmark. A daughter married the King of Norway.
3 Princess Alice (1843–78) married the Duke of Hesse-Darmstadt, and was the first of Victoria's children to die, of diphtheria. A daughter, Alix, married the ill-fated Tsar Nicholas II of Russia, and was assassinated with him and other members of the Russian royal family at Ekaterinburg (Sverdlovsk) in 1918. A granddaughter of Princess Alice married a future King of Sweden; the late Lord Louis Mountbatten was her grandson and HRH Prince Philip, Duke of Edinburgh, is her great-grandson.
4 Prince Alfred, Duke of Edinburgh (1844–1900), married Marie, daughter of Tsar Alexander II. A daughter married the King of Romania. A granddaughter married the King of Yugoslavia.

Queen Victoria and members of the royal family, c.1872 *(Hulton–Deutsch Collection)*.

5 Princess Helena (1846–1923) married Prince Christian of Schleswig-Holstein (German principality).
6 Princess Louise (1848–1939) married Lord Lorne, heir to the Duke of Argyll.
7 Prince Arthur, Duke of Connaught (1850–1942) married Princess Louise of Prussia.
8 Prince Leopold, Duke of Albany (1853–84), married Princess Helena of Waldeck (German principality), and died of haemophilia.
9 Princess Beatrice (1857–1944) married Prince Henry of Battenburg. A daughter married Alfonso XIII, the last king of Spain.

Edward VII

Born Buckingham Palace 9 November 1841. Ascended throne 1901. Reigned 9 years.
Eldest son of Queen Victoria.
Married Alexandra of Denmark (1863).
Three sons, three daughters.
Died Buckingham Palace 6 May 1910, aged 68. Buried at Windsor.

Edward was the first heir born to a reigning monarch since 1762. He was educated privately, and at the universities of Edinburgh, Christ Church, Oxford, and Trinity, Cambridge. Attempts to reduce the isolation that was inevitable in a royal upbringing by asking over boys from Eton had to be abandoned because of Edward's brutal behaviour to them. Later in life he would still take sadistic pleasure from stubbing out a cigar butt on the hand of an unsuspecting guest. It was probably his unpredictability that led Sir Frederick Ponsonby to write that 'there can be no doubt that even his most intimate friends were all terrified of him'.

Even after the death of his father in 1861 he was consistently denied any share in government, for his mother continued in the attitude of suspicion towards the heir-apparent which had marked all the rulers of Hanover. However, there was evidence enough of Edward's indiscretion, and Victoria's strong sense of duty was not reflected in any actions of Edward's. Victoria remained frozen in the grief and resentment she felt towards Edward when Albert died in 1861, deeply troubled on his deathbed by the liaison of Edward and an Irish actress while a guest of the cavalry on the Curragh in Ireland. It must have been hurtful to the Prince to see his mother instead take his sisters into her confidence. The Prince, denied an outlet for his energies, dissipated his great and growing powers in petty and unsuitable pursuits; after his marriage, he continued to have affairs which were public knowledge, the actress Lily Langtry, Lady Brooke and Mrs Keppel being amongst the best known of his mistresses; and he was involved in the Tranby Croft scandal, when a friend with whom the Prince was playing baccarat was accused of cheating, and the Mordaunt divorce case.

At the age of fifty-nine Edward VII, by then a grandfather, came to the throne. Many had shared Victoria's reservations about her son, largely due to his evident distaste for hard work and the intellectual pursuits that might have provided him with some knowledge of the empire whose sovereign he would become. It was soon apparent that Queen Victoria's usually sound judgement had been seriously at fault for, as king, Edward VII soon displayed skill in dealing with his ministers and with foreign rulers. Yet Edward's attempts to assert his influence, or at least the right to be consulted, were often rebuffed, particularly by Balfour who refused to discuss with him questions to be put to the Cabinet. But Edward continued the tradition of some predecessors in taking a particular interest in the armed services: he supported reforms, opposed cuts, backed Admiral Fisher's campaign for Dreadnoughts and played a prominent role in the creation of the Territorials, even summoning all the Lords-Lieutenant to Buckingham Palace to press them to make the force effective in their counties.

The field of foreign affairs was Edward's *forte*; what he lacked in knowledge from reading or questioning of ministers, he compensated for through his world-wide travels, made as Prince of Wales to Italy, Spain, America, Canada, India, Egypt and the Holy Land, Ireland, Denmark, France, Germany, Belgium and Russia. Speaking French and German fluently and Spanish and Italian adequately helped Edward to forge many useful links abroad. However, his visits were primarily useful for cementing personal relations and creating goodwill rather than having an impact on policy. If within two years of his accession he had become known as 'Edward the Peacemaker', this tribute to his constant attempts to foster international friendship was somewhat fanciful. Edward was still capable of the indiscretion and naivety that had discouraged Victoria from entrusting him with responsibilities: in 1901 he handed to the Kaiser the briefing notes Edward had been given for the meeting.

However, his genial disposition, active social life and popularity gave the monarchy a higher profile after the reclusiveness of so much of Victoria's reign. Even his extra-marital affairs were viewed tolerantly. Edward revived the custom of opening Parliament in person, which Victoria had given up, and restored some of the pageantry for which the British monarchy is admired.

Edward's involvement in domestic issues included being a member of the Housing Commission appointed by the Liberals in 1884. His questioning of witnesses illustrated that he was well aware of the difficulties faced by many men and women, and it was on the subject of housing that he made his only full speech to the Lords. Though his lifestyle suggested detachment from the poverty and squalor endured by many Britons, he was troubled by the extremes of wealth and poverty. Nor did his patriotism blind him to the injustices produced by the supercilious attitude of some privileged officials: when

Opposite: Edward VII: artist Sir Luke Fildes, date unknown *(The National Portrait Gallery, London)*.

visiting India in the 1870s he expressed strong disapproval of such conduct.

The reign of Edward VII saw important changes in England. During the last two decades of Queen Victoria's reign there had been a dearth of social legislation (successive Liberal and Conservative governments had been wrestling with the problem of Ireland, and Lord Salisbury did not believe in social improvement by legislation) and there was much headway to be made up. In 1902, an Education Act provided secondary education at the State's expense. The Liberal government after 1906 passed a series of reforms to benefit children, introduced old-age pensions (1908) and Labour Exchanges (1909), and laid the basis for the National Insurance scheme which was to be enacted early in the next reign. The money for these schemes was budgeted for in 1909, and the Lords' rejection of the Budget in that year sparked off a constitutional crisis.

The Chancellor responsible for the budget was Lloyd George, disliked by Edward since he had compared the costs of keeping a Duke and a Dreadnought (the battleship was cheaper). The Prime Minister, Asquith, demanded and got a dissolution of Parliament because of the Lords' veto, the first confrontation between the two houses over money for over two hundred years. Asquith asked Edward whether, if the Lords again rejected the Budget, he would create enough peers in the Lords to push through a Parliament Bill that would end the exercise of such power by the Lords. Recalling Victoria's belief that 'to threaten the House of Lords is, in fact, to threaten the monarchy itself', Edward agreed with great reluctance, provided that the issue was put to the country at a general election. The crisis was at its head when Edward died, leaving George V the unenviable task of resolving it.

During Edward's reign, the first Nobel prizes were awarded (1901), the world's first concentration camps were set up by Britain during the Boer War (1901), the Japanese routed the Russian navy and defeated the army through sheer weight of numbers during a two-year war (1904–5), signifying the emergence of a new power that threatened traditional empires, and the first buses driven by internal-combustion engines began operating in the streets of London.

A Saxe-Coburg by birth, upbringing and in appearance, Edward VII was really a Hanoverian. He possessed the social graces, shrewdness and care for personal appearance which had characterized that family; he set the fashions of the day. But he also had tact, kindness and warmth, qualities in which the Hanoverians had been markedly deficient. His affability and dandyism made him a popular figure with the majority of his subjects. Edward's sporting interests and activities had much to do with his popularity. His racing yacht *Britannia* was one of the most successful of her day, and the king had many wins on the turf. He became the first reigning monarch to win the Derby, with *Persimmon* in 1896, and won both the Derby and Grand National in 1900.

After Edward's accession, Edward's annual round was Christmas at Sandringham,

Edward VII: date unknown *(The Mansell Collection)*.

three or four weeks at Buckingham Palace, an avoidance of February or March weather in England by a spell in Biarritz, Easter at Windsor, the summer at Buckingham Palace broken up by breaks for Ascot and Goodwood and perhaps an official tour abroad; Cowes week would be followed by country-house visits for grouse-shooting, three weeks at a foreign spa in September, Balmoral for October and Buckingham Palace for the rest of the year, with a break at Sandringham for his birthday in November. Edward particularly enjoyed his time at Sandringham, the Norfolk house and estate bought for him in 1860. The house is architecturally unremarkable, but Edward was less interested in aesthetics than its potential for shooting, which was excellent.

Edward VII married Alexandra, eldest daughter of Christian IX of Denmark, in 1863. There were six children of the marriage: his eldest son, the Duke of Clarence, who died in 1892; the Duke of York, who succeeded his father as George V in 1910; the Princess Royal, who married the Duke of Fife; Princess Victoria; Princess Maud, who married King Haakon VII of Norway; and Alexander who was born and died in 1871.

King Edward died on 6 May 1910. Nine crowned heads of Europe followed him to his grave: the kings of England, Norway, Spain, Portugal, Belgium, Sweden and Denmark, the Tsar of Bulgaria and the Emperor of Germany. In addition, there were five heirs-apparent (including the ill-fated Archduke Franz Ferdinand of Austria*), seven queens and a host of minor royalty and foreign ambassadors, representing more than seventy different countries.

*See section on World War I, page 186.

George V

Born Marlborough House 3 June 1865. Ascended throne 1910. Reigned 25 years.
Second son of Edward VII.
Married Princess Mary of Teck (1893).
Five sons, one daughter.
Died Sandringham 20 January 1936, aged 70. Buried at Windsor.

The new king was the second son of Edward VII. Without expectation of succeeding to the throne, he was educated as a professional naval officer and saw service throughout the world. The death of his elder brother, the Duke of Clarence and Avondale, in 1892, forced him to relinquish his active naval career and assume the duties of heir-apparent.

In 1893, the Duke of York, as he now was, married his cousin, Princess Mary of Teck (1867–1953). The Princess, better known at this time as Princess May, was the daughter of Francis, Duke of Teck, a minor penurious German prince, and Mary Adelaide, the daughter of the Duke of Cambridge, seventh son of George III. She had been engaged to George's elder brother, but two months after the engagement he caught influenza and pneumonia and died at Sandringham. Her marriage to George proved felicitous. Throughout George's reign and after his death, Queen Mary was noted for her dedication to the interests of women and children, and for her general philanthropic work.

As a wedding present Edward VII gave them York Cottage, formerly known as Bachelor's Cottage and built as an annexe for male guests at Sandringham. Too small for the entertaining George V so disliked, he was particularly attached to its low-key domesticity, Mary less so, but they continued to live there until 1925. Harold Nicolson remarked that 'the rooms inside . . . are indistinguishable from those of any Surbiton or Upper Norwood home'. George's recreations were shooting (he was an excellent shot) and stamp collecting, and he dreaded public ceremonies. Allowed access to State papers by Edward VII that Edward himself that he had been denied as Prince of Wales, George acquired a fuller knowledge of the nation's affairs, augmented by his extensive travels, though he spoke no foreign language.

George V succeeded to the throne in the middle of a constitutional crisis. The Lords, containing a preponderance of Tory peers, had rejected the radical Liberal budget of 1909, the 'People's Budget'. This was an unprecedented act and the Liberals were seeking to restrict the powers of the Lords by Act of Parliament. After two elections in 1910 (the only year this has occurred in British history), George V was induced to agree to create sufficient Liberal peers to ensure the passage of the Parliament Bill in the House of Lords, should it be necessary. He strongly resented the pressure that he had been put under, not helped by contradictory opinions from his advisers.

George V: Coronation Portrait *(Hulton–Deutsch Collection)*.

Rather than be swamped by new Liberal peers, sufficient Conservatives stayed away or voted with the Liberals for the Bill to become law. The Parliament Bill prevented the Lords' rejection of any money bill, limited their power to block a bill to three successive occasions, after which it would automatically become law, and reduced the length of a Parliament from seven to five years.

Having become in the second election dependent upon the Irish members for a working majority, the Liberals opened up the prospect of Irish Home Rule. Both sides began armed preparation in Ireland, as there was no longer any possibility of the Lords blocking it for any length of time. The new Conservative leader, Bonar Law, suggested to George V that the royal veto might be used, but as one Liberal minister sagely advised, royal interference of that kind might 'reduce the throne to a hopeless ruin'. Talks in 1914 between Asquith and Bonar Law achieved nothing; a conference hosted by Buckingham Palace, which was resented by Radicals and Irish nationalists, collapsed over the issue of the borders of a separate Ulster. The outbreak of World War I only postponed the agony.

During World War I the king made several visits to the front line in France and Belgium. He was a war casualty himself: during a visit to France in 1915, his horse rolled on him and he received serious internal injuries from which he never fully recovered. The war enabled the king and queen to come into close contact with the mass of their people, to an extent unknown since the seventeenth century. Given the strong anti-German feelings in Britain, expressed arbitrarily to anyone with a foreign-sounding name, it was considered a propitious moment for the royal family to change its surname from Guelph (or Welf) and the House of Saxe-Coburg-Gotha to Windsor.

The survival, even the enhanced prestige, of the monarchy as a result of World War I occasions no comment by many historians, but of all wars it marked the end of monarchy as a feature of the hierarchy in most countries. This was partly because the royal family was closely identified with the war effort, but also because the nature of the monarchy's constitutional position was radical in comparison with the autocracies of Europe. The refusal of the British monarchy to be tarred with the brush of unreformed autocrats was reflected in the denial of asylum to the Russian royal family, despite Nicholas II being a cousin of George V; few could have anticipated their execution. A measure of the wide regard for the royal family, even after the shock waves of the Bolshevik Revolution, was that a Labour Party Conference motion that the royal family was no longer a necessary part of the constitution was defeated by a ratio of 10 votes to 1. Of course, part of the affection for the monarchy may be said to stem precisely from the turbulence and rapidity of change in so many areas of modern life, making it a symbol of continuity. Also the spread of the cinema made George V better known to the people of Britain than any previous monarch.

When the war ended the king was fifty-three, with another seventeen years of his reign left and innumerable crises and problems to overcome. The post-war years saw much social unrest and trouble in Ireland. The 'Sinn Fein' ('Ourselves Alone') Easter Rising of 1916, when the Irish Republican Army tried to create an independent state by force, was followed by a general election in 1918 at which Sinn Fein won seventy-three seats. They would not take them up at Westminster, forming instead a provisional government. British troops tried to suppress it, but negotiations between Lloyd George and Irish leaders produced the Government of Ireland Act, 1920, allowing for assemblies in Dublin and Belfast, divided on religious lines. In 1921 the king and queen visited Belfast to inaugurate the Northern Ireland Parliament. Following further armed resistance to achieve fuller independence than provided for by the 1920 Act, an agreement was reached the following year to set up the Irish Free State in the south, having Dominion status.

Social and industrial unrest resulted in the formation of the first Socialist government, which held office for a brief period, although in a minority in the Commons, in 1924. The Prime Minister was Ramsay Macdonald. In 1926, the General Strike took place: a sympathetic strike by the transport trade unions in support of the Miners' Federation brought the country to a halt. The strike lasted from 4 to 13 May, caused the loss of about 160 million working days and involved over 2 million employees. During the strike broadcast news bulletins, which replaced newspapers, proved the importance that radio was to have. The BBC had been established in 1926, and in 1937 the famous Christmas Day broadcast by the monarch was inaugurated.

The world economic crisis of 1929–31 had a drastic effect on Britain; there was a phenomenal rise in the number of unemployed and the finances of the country were on the verge of collapse. George V was instrumental in persuading the leaders of the three political parties – Ramsay Macdonald (Labour), Stanley Baldwin (Conservative) and Sir Herbert Samuel (Liberal) – to form a National Coalition government in August 1931, under the premiership of Macdonald. This was an extension of George's desire to act as mediator between the parties and the strongly divergent views of the time; as Harold Nicolson put it, 'unfalteringly and assiduously he sought to create a good blood'.

Not the least important feature of George V's reign was the change in the relationship between Britain and the other members of the Empire. This grew from a demand for self-government in New Zealand and the newly formed South Africa. (Following the two Boer Wars, in part over the refusal of the Boers to grant political rights to foreigners in the Transvaal and the Orange Free State, the Union of South Africa was established in the first month of George's reign, comprising the two Boer states and the previously British provinces of the Cape of Good Hope and Natal.)

Prior to 1914, the foreign policy of the Empire was determined by the British government, but after the war Dominion ministers began to express their determination that the imperial system must undergo radical change, so as to allow the whole Empire

George V: artist Lance Calkin, c1914 *(The National Portrait Gallery, London)*.

George V: military bust, 1914 *(Hulton–Deutsch Collection)*.

some voice in policies which affected the whole. The principle of Dominion independence was gradually accepted, and it received statutory definition in 1931, when the Statute of Westminster created the British Commonwealth of Nations. The Dominions were now no longer a group of colonies subordinated to England, but a Commonwealth of free nations. Outside the Commonwealth were still the Colonies, as distinct from the Dominions, and India. The last was accorded a measure of self-government in the Government of India Act, 1935, as the beginning of a transitional period which ended with the granting of India's independence in 1947. George V was, incidentally, the first reigning sovereign to visit India, when he attended a Durbar at Delhi in 1911, followed by a fortnight's big game shooting in Nepal.

George V and Queen Mary's six children were Prince Edward (Edward VIII); Prince Albert (George VI); Princess Mary, the Princess Royal (died 1965); Prince Henry (the Duke of Gloucester); Prince George (the Duke of Kent, killed in an air crash in 1942); and Prince John (died 1919).

George V celebrated his Silver Jubilee amidst vast crowds around the Palace in May 1935 and died of influenza on 20 January 1936. He was succeeded by his eldest son as Edward VIII.

Edward VIII

Born White Lodge, Richmond 23 June 1894. Ascended throne 20 January 1936.
Abdicated 11 December 1936. He was never crowned.
Eldest son of George V.
Married Mrs Wallis Simpson (1937).
No issue.
Died Paris 28 May 1972, aged 77. Buried at Windsor.

Edward VIII became king on 20 January 1936, and was to have the shortest reign in the country's history, with the exception of that of his namesake, Edward V.

Called David by his family, Prince Edward later regarded his childhood at York Cottage on the Sandringham estate as having been unhappy; the evidence points to a delightfully carefree time until dispatched to the Royal Naval Colleges at Osborne and Dartmouth. Yet after eight terms at Oxford, the Prince went into the Grenadier Guards, serving on the Western Front where he was kept well out of harm's way. After a period in the navy, Edward travelled extensively, making successful official visits to Canada, the United States, New Zealand, Australia and India; Lloyd George called the Prince 'our greatest ambassador', though the Prince's predeliction for unofficial nocturnal companions caused concern. Always under the scrutiny of his father, whose letters sometimes upbraided him for a minor sartorial solecism, the Prince was cast in the mould of his grandfather, preferring the life of the smart set at nightclubs to anything that might be regarded as preparation for becoming king. Though his physical appearance and charm won praise, he was never able to conceal boredom, and would sometimes start chatting about racing or other subjects congenial to him in the middle of an important meeting. He disliked the ceremonial aspects of monarchy, and tried to reduce such commitments.

Before the death of George V, rumours were circulating of an attachment which the Prince of Wales had formed, and after the accession as king these grew in volume, particularly in American and Continental newspapers; the British press had agreed between themselves to ignore the subject. The details of this relationship with Mrs Wallis Simpson were kept from the British public for a remarkably long time.

Mrs Simpson, born Wallis Warfield, was the daughter of a Baltimore family with old and aristocratic connections in Maryland and Virginia. She had divorced her first husband, Lt Winfield Spencer of the US navy, in 1927, and married in the same year Mr Ernest Simpson, a London stockbroker of Anglo-American parentage. The Prince had met Mrs Simpson in 1930, and she first visited his house within Windsor Great Park, Fort Belvedere, in 1932. By 1934 his former consorts, Lady Furness and Mrs Dudley Ward, had been dropped to devote more time to Mrs Simpson. Though the king and Mrs Simpson went on holiday together to the Balkans in the summer of 1936 and they were much photographed by press photographers, the newspapers still maintained a silence. It was only when Bishop Blunt of Bradford hinted in a sermon that the king might be neglecting his spiritual responsibilities and the *Yorkshire Post* looked for a reason behind Dr Blunt's comments that the story broke.

With the news that Mrs Simpson was filing a divorce petition the crisis was at hand. Stanley Baldwin tried to defuse it during an audience when he warned the king of the possible hazards and the feeling that the relationship was engendering in the country. The leaders of the Liberal and Labour parties concurred with Baldwin's view that Mrs Simpson would be unacceptable as queen. On 27 October 1936 she was granted a decree nisi, and it became clear that the king intended to marry her. Constitutionally the king could marry whom he wished; but if he did so against the advice of his Cabinet, and the Cabinet resigned over the issue, there would be a general election which would be damaging to the concept of constitutional monarchy.

Edward was not without support, though some of it came from quarters that were not likely to encourage others or do the king's cause much good; others supported him for reasons that had little to do with the fundamental issues. The newspaper barons Lords Rothermere and Beaverbrook supported a morganatic settlement, and Churchill pleaded in the Commons for a delay. There were demonstrations outside Buckingham Palace that united Communists and Fascists, and it was reported that about sixty MPs were willing to support a king's government.

There were in theory four courses open to the king: he could marry Mrs Simpson and make her queen; he could contract a morganatic marriage – that is, neither Mrs Simpson nor any issue of the marriage would share in the royal status or property; he could abdicate and then marry; he could abandon Mrs Simpson.

The national objection to Mrs Simpson was not that she was an American, nor that she was a commoner. Both Edward IV and Henry VIII had married commoners, as had the king's own brother, the future George VI. But Mrs Simpson had divorced two husbands, both of whom were still alive; and although there was a royal precedent for a king's marriage to a divorced person – that of Henry II to Eleanor of Aquitaine – the idea was disliked. Marriage to a divorced person would raise in acute form the question of the king's relationship to the established Church, whose official doctrine censured the whole concept of divorce. Moreover, it still carried a stigma that could end public careers of lesser mortals than a king. English law did not recognize any such thing as a morganatic marriage, so Edward VIII's choice was between abandonment of the throne or of the woman he loved.

Relations between the king and Mrs Simpson formed the only topic of conversation throughout the British Isles, despite the plight of 2 million unemployed, Mosley and the Fascists, the Spanish Civil War and the threat of Hitler on the Continent. It was well said at the time that Hitler might have seized Austria without the British public either knowing or caring.

Denied the possibility of a morganatic marriage by the Cabinet, Edward informed Baldwin that he wished to make a broadcast that would effectively have complained of his treatment by the government. When this was refused, the king conceded the inevitability of abdication and made a broadcast announcing his decision and the reasons for it on 11 December 1936. He asked the country to support his brother Albert, and left England from Portsmouth aboard the destroyer HMS *Fury*. On the previous day, by the Declaration of Abdication Act, Edward VIII formally renounced his throne and was succeeded by his brother, the Duke of York, as George VI; one of the first new king's acts was to create the ex-king Duke of Windsor.

The Duke of Windsor and Mrs Simpson were married in 1937, but Mrs Simpson was refused the title of Royal Highness. It was a denial that was to rankle Edward for the rest of his life, referring to it as 'a kind of Berlin Wall alienating us from my family'. Given a handsome annuity by George VI in return for relinquishing his life interest in Balmoral and Sandringham and their contents, the Duke led a somewhat resentful and self-indulgent exile in comfortable circumstances. They lived mostly in Paris, where the City provided an elegant house in the Bois de Boulogne, though during World War II Edward was Governor of the Bahamas after a short period with the British Military

Opposite: Edward VIII: artist P. G. Eves *(The National Portrait Gallery, London).*

Mission in France and six weeks in Spain, where he indiscreetly forecast Britain's defeat. His pre-war expressions of admiration for Germany did not endear him to those who could foresee the makings of catastrophe. Post-war life in France was filled with golf, gardening and cairn terriers. The Duchess of Windsor was not received by the royal family until Elizabeth II relented on the occasion of the dedication of a memorial to Queen Mary. Mrs Simpson died in 1986 and is buried beside her husband at Frogmore.

Edward VIII: photographed when he was Prince of Wales *(Hulton–Deutsch Collection)*.

George VI

Born Sandringham 14 December 1895. Ascended throne 1936.
Reigned 15 years.
Second son of George V.
Married Lady Elizabeth Bowes-Lyon (1923).
Two daughters.
Died Sandringham 6 February 1952, aged 56. Buried at Windsor.

Like his father George VI had not expected to become king. Known as 'Bertie' to the family – he was christened Albert Frederick Arthur George – Prince Albert's childhood was clouded by illness and a stammer he developed at eight. Educated at Dartmouth Naval College and Trinity College, Cambridge, Prince Albert served during World War I aboard HMS *Collingwood,* seeing action during the Battle of Jutland (1916). Invalided out, he became an air cadet at Cranwell and was a talented tennis player, winning the Royal Air Force doubles and in 1926 playing at Wimbledon in the All-England Championships. After the war he became closely involved with the problems of human relations in industry, giving his patronage to the Industrial Welfare Society and becoming president of the Boys' Welfare Association, establishing the Duke of York's boys camps for public school and working-class boys.

George's marriage in 1923, described as the wisest decision of his life, was made possible by his father's relaxation of the policy on royal marriages, for his wife, the Lady Elizabeth Bowes-Lyon, though a direct descendant of the kings of Scotland, was a commoner; George had been the first prince (but not princess) of royal blood to marry a commoner since the reign of George III. As George VI's official biographer wrote, 'the Duchess was not only to be the partner of his happiness but his inspiration and encouragement in the face of adversity, his enduring source of strength in joy and sadness. Hers was the ability to sustain or reward him by a single smile or gesture in the public battles he waged with his stammer; hers the capacity to calm with a word that passionate temper which every now and again would burst its bounds.' In 1927 the Duke and Duchess went on a long tour of Australia and New Zealand.

The new king needed all the support he could get. The prestige of the throne was lower than at any time since the accession of Queen Victoria. Soon after his accession, George wrote that he hoped he would be allowed sufficient time 'to make amends for what has happened'. The abdication crisis would have figured more prominently in British history had it not been over so quickly as far as the public was concerned and because it was so soon overshadowed by the outbreak of World War II. However, it was soon apparent that George VI had inherited the steady virtues which had distinguished his father and endeared him to the English people.

George VI: artist P. G. Eves, 1924 *(The National Portrait Gallery, London)*.

Elizabeth (Queen Mother): artist Sir Gerald Kelly, c1938 *(The National Portrait Gallery, London)*.

George VI had hoped to hold a durbar following his coronation, but it never proved politically expedient. However, in 1938 the king and queen visited France, and in the summer of 1939 Canada and the United States. Shortly after the coronation, Neville Chamberlain took over from Stanley Baldwin as Prime Minister; George favoured Chamberlain's policy of appeasement, as did many at the time, and even suggested personal appeals to Hitler, the Italian king and Japanese emperor, an idea not endorsed by the Cabinet. With the outbreak of war, Chamberlain's shortcomings as a wartime leader became apparent and he was compelled to resign after the failure of the Norway expedition. The king at first favoured the Foreign Secretary Lord Halifax as Chamberlain's successor, but being in the Lords, Halifax felt that he would be at arm's

George VI and family: Royal Lodge, Windsor 1940 *(Hulton–Deutsch Collection)*.

length from the Commons. The king later wrote: 'Then I knew that there was only one person I could send for to form a Government who had the confidence of the country, and that was Winston.' At first the relationship between the King and Winston Churchill was cool, but formal meetings soon gave way to a weekly lunch at the Palace to discuss the latest developments in the war, and Churchill entrusted the king with the most guarded secrets. He was one of only four people to know the detailed plans for the use of the atom bomb.

The war enhanced the importance of the throne, as it had done in George V's time. When it began, King George VI and Queen Elizabeth were little more than constitutional abstractions; by the time it had finished they were firmly entrenched in the nation's affections. The king and queen set an example of fortitude, raising morale by visiting troops, munitions factories, docks and bomb-damaged areas, freely showing their concern for people under stress. It was these peregrinations through bomb-scarred streets that gave the king the idea for the George Cross and the George Medal. They refused to leave Buckingham Palace, even though it was directly hit by a bomb while they were in the building, thereby expressing their willingness to share with Londoners the nightly terror of the Blitz. The king also visited the front line in North Africa, Malta and Italy.

After the war the emergency coalition, led by Winston Churchill, was replaced by Britain's third Socialist government under the leadership of Clement Attlee. The king was deeply disappointed by the country's rejection of the man who had done so much to secure victory, but he was not averse to the Labour manifesto on principle, supporting Attlee's intention of giving independence to India. However, he did think the nationalization of the Bank of England, the mines, railways, road transport, gas and electricity, the health services, and iron and steel too much for the country to assimilate in a single Parliament. But there were few problems with Attlee's administration, and the king was gratified by the Prime Minister's agreement that the three senior orders of chivalry (the Garter, the Thistle and St Patrick) should no longer be political rewards but the prerogative of the monarch.

In 1947 the king and queen toured South Africa and neighbouring Protectorates, the programme being so taxing that the king lost 17lb (7.6kg). Arteriosclerosis and lung cancer took their toll on the king's health, and he died in his sleep in February 1952 while Princess Elizabeth and Prince Philip were on the first leg of a visit to East Africa, Australia and New Zealand.

Like his father, George VI had a strong sense of duty, a great respect for tradition and continuity and was a stickler for dress. Before the annual trooping the colour, he would wear the Brigade of Guards bearskin cap while gardening to accustom himself to its weight.

George VI was succeeded by his eldest daughter as Elizabeth II.

Elizabeth II

Born 17 Bruton Street, London WI, 21 April 1926. Ascended throne 1952.
Elder daughter of George VI.
Married Philip Mountbatten, RN, formerly Prince Philip of
Schleswig-Holstein-Sonderburg-Glucksburg (1947)
Three sons, one daughter.

When Princess Elizabeth was born at the London home of the Duchess of York's parents, there was little expectation that she would become queen; the Prince of Wales was then only thirty-one and there was every possibility that her parents would have a son who would take precedence. Edward VIII's abdication made her heir presumptive. As a child she captivated those around her with her quick intelligence and relaxed formality; during a visit to Balmoral when Princess Elizabeth was two, Sir Winston Churchill wrote that 'she has an air of authority and reflectiveness astonishing in an infant'. Later, when Princess Elizabeth was sixteen, Lady Airlie noted that 'there was about her that indescribable something which Queen Victoria had'.

Educated privately, Princess Elizabeth spent much of the war at Windsor Castle, and became a subaltern in the ATS. Given the very changed prospects for her future, courses in constitutional history and the French language, literature and history were added to the curriculum. After the war she accompanied her parents on their 1947 tour of South Africa, and it was in Cape Town that she celebrated her twenty-first birthday, making a broadcast speech of dedication to the Commonwealth.

On their return from South Africa, the engagement was announced of Princess Elizabeth to her third cousin Lieutenant Philip Mountbatten (see p 157) whom the Princess had first met at Dartmouth Naval College in July 1939 and corresponded with throughout the war. The wedding in November 1947 was a relaxation from the post-war austerity, providing a day of pageantry and colour; Princess Elizabeth had been given an extra 100 clothing coupons for her satin dress. The honeymoon was at Broadlands, the Hampshire home of Lord and Lady Mountbatten, and at Birkhall on the Balmoral estate. There are four children of the marriage: Prince Charles, born 14 November 1948; Princess Anne, born 15 August 1950; Prince Andrew, born 19 February 1960; and Prince Edward, born 10 March 1964.

Princess Elizabeth was only twenty-five when she and Prince Philip were recalled from their royal tour in Kenya on the death of King George VI. Her independence was asserted in the preparations for the coronation on 2 June 1953 when she insisted against the advice of the Prime Minister Sir Winston Churchill, the Cabinet and the Archbishop of Canterbury that the ceremony be televised. It was watched by 20 million and heard by 12 million people.

George VI and Princess Elizabeth: Royal Lodge, Windsor 1942 *(Hulton–Deutsch Collection)*.

Queen Elizabeth's accession was accompanied by a constitutional innovation: she was proclaimed in each of the self-governing countries of what used to be called the British Empire as Queen of that particular country. The formal abandonment of the principle of the indivisibility of the Crown was confirmed by statute in 1953, and a new description, 'Head of the Commonwealth', was inserted amongst the royal titles to allow for the inclusion of republics like India and Pakistan. A feature of the reign has been the number of independent states which have come into being, the Commonwealth in 1986 comprising forty-nine states.

The Queen's role as Head of the Commonwealth has taken her on numerous tours of member states, one of the most notable being the 56,000 mile tour of Commonwealth countries in 1977, the year of the Queen's Silver Jubilee. She is also responsible for the appointment of Governors-General on the advice of the particular country's prime minister. The Queen's concern for the Commonwealth and her position as its head is reflected in her ire over the cavalier invasion of Grenada, of which she is head of state, by the United States in 1983; as a close ally, the least that might have been expected was notification of its intentions. The strains imposed upon relations within the Commonwealth by Prime Minister Thatcher's refusal to agree to economic sanctions against South Africa has also been a source of concern to the Queen.

Elizabeth II, and the royal family as a whole, has played a much more strenuous role in the life of the nation and Commonwealth. The continual round of state visits, overseas tours, attendance at all manner of events within Britain, and entertaining of guests from all walks of life has placed a much greater burden on the monarch than on her predecessors. The strain of being forever in the public eye and the focus of countless press and television cameras has meant that those times when it has been possible to relax with her family are rarer and more precious than for previous monarchs. Resentment of the *papparazzi*'s intrusion on such moments has fuelled debate over the role of the tabloid press in depriving the royal family of what little privacy they enjoy.

Though the theoretical powers of the monarch remain considerable – Bagehot cited examples such as disbanding the army and navy, creating a universal peerage in the kingdom and dismissing the civil service – Queen Elizabeth's exercise of them is limited to that of a constitutional sovereign who has to abide by the advice of ministers on government policy. But the resignation of two Conservative prime ministers has placed the Queen in the position of choosing a successor. When Anthony Eden resigned in 1957, Harold Macmillan was appointed by the Queen in preference to R. A. Butler, who had deputized for Eden's absences due to ill-health. This occasioned surprise amongst the public but not amongst the Cabinet and others whose opinions were canvassed, such as Churchill. The resignation of Macmillan in 1963, again on the grounds of ill-health, produced a greater choice of candidates; the Queen followed the advice of

Macmillan in sending for Lord Home as the most acceptable choice for the whole party. This awkward situation cannot arise again, as the Conservative Party has followed the Labour Party in establishing a system for choosing their leaders.

The royal family have of course been affected by the post-war change in social outlook and habits; their frequent travels, with Prince Philip's cheerful informality and hard work for good causes, have done much to identify them with the everyday life of the nation. Some of the anachronisms of court life have been done away with, such as the presentation of debutantes and the refusal of admission into the royal enclosure at Ascot even of innocent parties to a divorce case. At the same time, in an age of recurrent international crises and economic problems, the monarchy's stability and the pageantry still surrounding it have remained a valuable focal point for the nation's self-respect and sense of identity.

The Queen's principal recreation has been horses, attending race meetings, often to watch her own horses compete; but the aspect that interests her most is breeding and training, and she has been on private visits to the United States to look at stud farms.

In 1965 Sir Winston Churchill died, one of Britain's greatest statesmen; he was given what will probably be the last lavish state funeral. He had served six monarchs and held a variety of high offices from 1905 to 1955, when he retired as Prime Minister, but he will be remembered most for his brilliant leadership during World War II.

Prince Philip, Duke of Edinburgh

Prince Philip was born in Corfu, Greece, on 10 June 1921. He was the fifth child and only son of Princess Alice of Battenburg (a great-granddaughter of Queen Victoria) and Prince Andrew of Greece. Prince Andrew owed his life to British intervention. In 1922, after the Greek disaster in Asia Minor at the hands of the Turks, the Greek ministers in office were executed; Prince Andrew, who had commanded the right wing of the Greek army, was awaiting trial with the certainty of the death sentence following. An unofficial ambassador was sent to Athens and succeeded in securing his release. Prince Andrew's eighteen-month-old son Philip is said to have been brought on board in an orange box.

From 1923 to 1935, the Greek royal family was in exile in England. Prince Philip was educated at Cheam School, Gordonstoun and the Royal Naval College, Dartmouth, and spent much of his childhood in England under the guardianship of his maternal uncle, the 2nd Marquess of Milford Haven. During World War II he saw active service with the Royal Navy and he served on the battleship HMS *Valiant* at the battle of Cape Matapan (1941). He later took part in the Sicily landings and was aboard the American battleship *Missouri* when the Japanese surrendered in Tokyo Bay.

He became a British subject in February 1947, renouncing his Greek titles and membership of the Greek Orthodox Church, and adopted the name of Mountbatten, the

Above: Elizabeth II: artist Pietro Annigoni, 1969 *(The National Portrait Gallery, London)*.

Elizabeth II taking the salute at the Trooping the Colour *(Daily Telegraph Colour Library)*.

anglicized form of his mother's family name of Battenburg. The day before he married Princess Elizabeth, George VI conferred on him the title of Duke of Edinburgh and the qualification of 'His Royal Highness'. In 1957, the Duke was granted the titular dignity of Prince of the United Kingdom.

After his marriage, the Duke of Edinburgh returned to his naval career, becoming commander of the frigate HMS *Magpie*. He has continued his interest in the Services and holds numerous important appointments, including Admiral of the Fleet and Marshal of the Royal Air Force. He has continued George VI's interest and work in industrial relations and developments, being Patron of the Industrial Society and the sponsor of six international study conferences on the human problems of industrial societies. The Duke of Edinburgh awards scheme reflects his interest in the capacity of young people to play a role in community service, develop their appreciation of outdoor recreation and test their self-reliance.

Prince Philip is well known for his concern for the environment; he has spoken out strongly on the threats posed by man to the world's fragile ecology and the dangers of ignoring the mounting evidence of serious environmental damage. He has been closely involved with the World Wildlife Fund since 1961, and is President of the renamed World Wide Fund for Nature. His recreations include four-in-hand driving and polo, and he is a qualified pilot, regularly taking the controls of aircraft in the Queen's Flight.

The Prince of Wales

Prince Charles Philip Arthur George, Prince of Wales and Earl of Chester,
Duke of Cornwall, Duke of Rothesay, Earl of Carrick and Baron Renfrew.
Lord of the Isles and Great Steward of Scotland.
Born 14 November 1948 at Buckingham Palace, the eldest son of Queen Elizabeth II
and HRH Prince Philip.
Married Lady Diana Spencer.
Two sons.

HRH Prince Charles was created Prince of Wales and Earl of Chester on 26 July 1958. His investiture as Prince of Wales took place on 1 July 1969 at Caernarfon Castle. He is the twenty-first holder of the title.

Many radical decisions were made by his parents with regard to education and upbringing to fit him for a supposedly egalitarian society. He was the first heir to the throne to be educated outside the royal homes. After preparatory school he went on to the school his father had attended, at Gordonstoun, Scotland, where he learned to adapt himself to the rigorous conditions which were to fit him for his chosen Royal Navy career. However, Prince Charles is believed to have disliked the spartan regime with its emphasis on character building at the expense of more intellectual pursuits. He also spent a period in Australia at Timbertop, an outpost in the Victorian Alps of the Geelong Church of England Grammar School, the Australian equivalent of Eton, afterwards travelling extensively round the country, including spending a week in the Snowy Mountains with the Queen Mother. He was at Trinity College, Cambridge, from 1967 to 1969 and later at the University College of Wales before graduating as BA (Cantab) in June 1970. He is the first Prince of Wales to have gained a university degree.

Prince Charles is a well-qualified pilot and helicopter pilot. He served with the RAF in 1971 and later transferred to the navy, eventually commanding the coastal mine-hunter HMS *Bronington* based at Rosyth, Scotland. His service career continued until December 1976 when he left the Royal Navy, having served in the West Indies, Singapore and the Arctic, interrupted by other visits.

He has represented the Queen on many occasions, the first being in 1967 at the memorial service of Harold Holt, Prime Minister of Australia. With a dedication and professionalism which impresses all who meet him, not least the ever-critical Press with whom he has established an excellent relationship based on mutual respect, he has enjoyed a breadth of experience unrivalled by any previous Prince of Wales. His thirst for excitement and adventure is apparent from the list of pursuits he has followed, including training as a frogman and commando, parachute jumping, hang-gliding and diving under icecaps. He has climbed the foothills of the Himalayas, dived for sunken treasure, and has ridden in many steeplechases. In addition he is an expert rifle shot and an excellent swimmer.

On the polo field – one of his particular pleasures – he is first class and like other members of the royal family loves horses and riding. Whilst obviously an outdoor man, he has many other interests such as music and painting. He has been an entertaining and forceful critic of architectural ill-manners and unimaginative commercial developments that give pleasure to no one but those who profit by them. He has also championed aspects of conservation that his father has not encompassed, such as the use of chemicals in farming and food production.

His sensibilities are reflected in the choice of Laurens van der Post as godfather to one of his sons. Prince Charles's obvious concern about the quality of life in Britain has won him admiration and respect from all quarters; it has resulted in his involvement with many organizations designed to improve opportunities for the underprivileged, such as The Prince's Youth Business Trust, The Prince's Trust, The Prince of Wales' Community Venture and The Prince of Wales' Advisory Group on Disability.

Prince Charles has no income from the State. He heads the organization which administers the estates of the Duchy of Cornwall. Comprising some 130,000 acres, it makes him one of the largest landowners in the country. His home outside London is Highgrove House in Gloucestershire, bought from the late son of Harold Macmillan.

Prince Philip enjoying one of his favourite sports – carriage driving *(Daily Telegraph Colour Library)*.

Above: HRH The Duke of Edinburgh *(Daily Telegraph Colour Library)*.

Below: HRH The Prince of Wales, heir to the throne *(Daily Telegraph Colour Library)*.

The Princess of Wales

Diana Frances Spencer.
Born 1 July 1961 at Park House on her father's property on the Sandringham estate.
Daughter of 8th Earl Spencer and the Hon Mrs Peter Shand Kydd.
Two sons.

The Earl Spencer, educated at Eton and Sandhurst and a Guard's officer, served as equerry to King George VI and the present Queen. His home is the 15,000 acre estate at Althorp, Northamptonshire, a family seat for more than 450 years. The Earl can trace his ancestry back to the fifteenth century. Lady Diana and Prince Charles are 11th cousins once removed.

Lady Diana captured the hearts of the British public immediately the possibility of a royal engagement became known. Her natural dignity, when the Press and other media brought her under the spotlight of intense publicity which must have made her life unbearable, was greatly admired and she received the sympathy of the nation.

Though Lady Diana was brought up at her father's house on the Sandringham estate, it was probably not until 1977, when Prince Charles attended a shooting party at Althorp, that they met. Lady Diana was educated at private schools where she played tennis and lacrosse and was described as average academically. She left school at sixteen and attended Swiss finishing school for six months before arriving in London to start working with obvious enjoyment as an assistant at a private kindergarten in Pimlico – a role she was quietly pursuing until the outburst of publicity over her relationship with the Prince.

The Royal Wedding

The Engagement
The announcement of the engagement was made at 11am on Tuesday 24 February 1981, in the following style:

It is with the greatest pleasure that the Queen and the Duke of Edinburgh announce the betrothal of their beloved son, the Prince of Wales, to the Lady Diana Spencer, daughter of the Earl Spencer and the Honourable Mrs Shand Kydd.

History plays an important part in the marriage of a royal heir. When the announcement had been made by the Palace, the Queen had to give her formal assent to the marriage. This she must do under the Royal Marriage Act that was passed in 1772 by George III who disapproved of the marriages made by his two brothers.

The Queen assented to the marriage of her son and Lady Diana at a meeting of the

Privy Council, following which a document, or instrument, was drawn up for the Queen's signature. The instrument was sealed with the Great Seal of England – the mark of authenticity on all important government documents. Dating from late Anglo–Saxon times, the Great Seal, which weighs over 8lb (3.6kg) and is recast for each reign, was taken to Buckingham Palace from its home in the House of Lords. Only when the sovereign's formal assent had been given could the marriage take place.

Overall responsibility for the organization of royal weddings rests with the Lord Chamberlain, Lord Maclean, who was appointed to the office in 1972, and organized the wedding of Prince Charles's sister, Princess Anne, to Captain Mark Phillips at Westminster Abbey.

The marriage of Lady Diana to Prince Charles was the first time for more than 300 years that the heir to the throne of England has married a British subject. The last time this happened was in 1659, when Charles II's brother James, later James II, married Lady Anne Hyde, elder daughter of the 1st Earl of Clarendon. The same situation nearly arose in 1785 when the then Prince of Wales, who later became George IV, secretly married his great love, a widow – Mary Anne Fitzherbert; but because in law, marriage to a Catholic entailed the heir's forfeiting his right of succession to the throne, the marriage was declared invalid, and George subsequently married Caroline of Brunswick.

On her marriage Lady Diana became Princess of Wales. Her predecessor in this rank was the wife of George V, who became Queen Mary in 1910.

The Wedding

The wedding took place on 29 July 1981. Britain had suffered a dismal summer with very few sunny and warm days but fortune smiled on the happy couple and produced a beautiful day.

Never before in history had there been such a 'public' wedding; so great was the interest all over the world that it is estimated that including those of the Commonwealth a total of fifty countries, from Poland to Indonesia, watched and listened for hours on end. The audience totalled some thousand million people.

In London some people began camping out along the wedding route more than forty-eight hours before to secure vantage points for the pageantry which only Britain with its long tradition can mount with such expertise. It was a day of colour and warmth that was perfect in every way. The streets of London were thronged with an estimated million people and never were there such good-humoured crowds. Full of fun they turned out to line the processional routes to laugh, sing and cheer.

They were well rewarded for there were three processions travelling from Buckingham Palace to St Paul's Cathedral, all in the full panoply of state with beautiful horses, historic carriages and the shining breastplates and plumed helmets of the

Above: HRH The Prince of Wales at the Trooping the Colour *(Daily Telegraph Colour Library)*.
Opposite: Prince Charles off duty after a game of polo *(Daily Telegraph Colour Library)*.

Household Cavalry. The streets were lined with men of the three services and more than 5,000 police were on duty.

From Clarence House came a fourth procession – that of the bride accompanied by her father – which was escorted only by mounted police for she was then still a commoner.

The wedding dress had been kept a complete secret and was first seen fully when she stepped from her coach at St Paul's to be greeted by a roar of welcome from the assembled crowds. It was indeed a fairytale dress, with a boned and fitted bodice of ivory silk paper taffeta and antique lace, hand-embroidered with tiny mother-of-pearls; a deep, gently curved neckline and billowing sleeves, both trimmed with bows and elaborately embroidered lace flounces to match the centre panel. The veil made from ivory silk tulle was spangled with ten thousand mother-of-pearl sequins and held in place by the magnificent Spencer family diamond tiara. The sweeping train, trimmed and edged with sparkling lace, was twenty-five feet long.

The bride was attended by five bridesmaids who, as is so often the case, almost stole the show. They were: Lady Sarah Armstrong-Jones aged seventeen; India Hicks, granddaughter of the late Lord Mountbatten; Sarah Jane Gaselee; Catherine Cameron; and Clementine Hambro, aged five, great granddaughter of Sir Winston Churchill to whom the Princess of Wales is related. There were two pages, Lord Nicholas Windsor, son of the Duke and Duchess of Kent, and Edward van Cutsem. The groom had previously arrived with his two brothers as supporters. By tradition, there was no best man.

The couple themselves chose St Paul's Cathedral as the venue, and to set the scene inside there was a red carpet stretching from the pavement to the High Altar, a distance of 652 feet. Inside the building there was a galaxy of colour, accentuated by the Yeomen of the Guard in their Tudor uniforms, the members of Her Majesty's Body Guard of the Honourable Corps of Gentlemen at Arms and the dresses and headgear of the 3,500 invited guests from many parts of the world. Placed in the Cathedral to relay every part of the service were twenty-two television cameras.

Many of the invited guests arrived some two hours before the ceremony was to begin. Apart from all the members of the British royal family, foreign guests included the Princess of Monaco, the Prince and Princess of Liechtenstein, the Grand Duke and Duchess of Luxembourg, the Queen and Prince Claus of the Netherlands, the King and Queen of Sweden, the Queen and Prince of Denmark, the King of Norway (Edward VII's last grandson), the Crown Prince and Princess of Norway and the King and Queen of the Belgians. Other heads of state included the President of the French Republic, M. Mitterrand, the first lady of America, Mrs Nancy Reagan, and the King of Tonga. The Ministers of the government were headed by Mrs Margaret Thatcher, Harold Macmillan, Sir Alec Douglas-Home, Sir Harold Wilson, Edward Heath and James Callaghan. Guests also included the three former flatmates of the bride and 200 workers from the royal estates who sat side by side with the famous of many lands.

In addition to the state trumpeters, three orchestras and the Bach choir took part in the service. The Prince of Wales, himself a keen musician, had paid special attention to the choice of music and it was indeed beautiful.

The service was conducted by the Archbishop of Canterbury, Primate of all England, assisted by the Dean of St Paul's, the Cardinal Archbishop of Westminister and the Moderator of the General Assembly of the Church of Scotland. The Right Honourable George Thomas, Speaker of the House of Commons, read the lesson.

On her return journey to the Palace, the bride, now Princess of Wales, ranked as the third lady of the land to whom all others except the Queen, Prince Philip and the Queen Mother must bow or curtsey. The carriages, all of them open, made their way through the hundreds of thousands of wildly cheering spectators.

When all had arrived at the Palace, the police, with superb organization and masterly control, allowed the vast crowd to filter into the Mall until it seemed as if every inch of space was filled, from the railings of the Palace back to Admiralty Arch. The crowd was in good humour and exuberant spirit and kept up a chant for the royal family to make their appearance on the balcony. Never before had a Prince kissed his bride publicly – a spontaneous gesture which was noted with wild delight by the crowd.

After the wedding breakfast the Prince and Princess drove in an open carriage escorted by Household Cavalry to Waterloo Station. Over Westminster Bridge the ships on the River Thames, the scene of medieval pageantry in the past, sounded their sirens. A special train took the couple to Hampshire where they spent a few days before joining the Royal Yacht *Britannia* at Gibraltar for a fortnight's cruising honeymoon.

For a nation in a period of severe economic gloom and depression and with grave social problems, the great event was taken as a reason to relax and rejoice. Never have the massive crowds shown such overwhelming and touching affection and enthusiasm and it was as if to demonstrate that patriotism and friendliness were back in fashion. The salute of the nation was not in deference to the monarchy but genuine respect and affection for a family that has adapted smoothly to the needs of our times.

Prince William was born in June 1982 and Prince Harry in September 1984.

Marriage of the Princess Anne

On 14 November 1973 Princess Anne was married to Capt Mark Phillips. They have two children, Peter (born 1977) and Zara (born 1981), and live at Gatcombe Park in Gloucestershire.

In September 1989, it was announced from Buckingham Palace that the Princess Royal and her husband had decided to part after fifteen years. The formal announcement from the Palace reads: 'Her Royal Highness, the Princess Royal, and Captain Mark

HRH The Princess of Wales: Sandhurst 1987 *(Daily Telegraph Colour Library)*.

Phillips have decided to separate on terms agreed between them. There are no plans for divorce proceedings.' The Princess's work on behalf of the Save the Children Fund has brought her much acclaim and it is a work that takes her all over the world. Captain Mark Phillips has business interests in the equestrian field and a business which also takes him abroad a great deal.

Marriage of the Prince Andrew

On 23 July 1986 Prince Andrew was married to Miss Sarah Ferguson, daughter of Major Ronald Ferguson and his former wife Mrs Hector Barrantes. They have one child, Beatrice (born 1988) and, at the time of writing, they are expecting the birth of their second child in the spring of 1990. This child will be 5th in line to the throne (if a boy) and 6th (if a girl) and the Royal Line of Succession (see page 172) will be altered accordingly.

The engagement of Prince Charles and Lady Diana Spencer *(Tim Graham Picture Library)*.

Royal Line of Succession

1. Prince of Wales (1948)
2. Prince William (1982)
3. Prince Harry (1984)
4. Prince Andrew (1960)
5. Princess Beatrice (1988)
6. Prince Edward (1964)
7. Princess Anne (1950)
8. Peter Phillips (1977)
9. Zara Phillips (1981)
10. Princess Margaret (1930)
11. Viscount Linley (1961)
12. Lady Sarah Armstrong-Jones (1963)
13. Duke of Gloucester (1944)
14. Earl of Ulster (1974)
15. Lady Davina Windsor (1977)
16. Lady Rose Windsor (1980)
17. Duke of Kent (1935)
18. Earl of St Andrews (1962)
19. Lord Nicholas Windsor (1970)
20. Lady Helen Windsor (1964)
21. Lord Frederick Windsor (1979)
22. Lady Ella Windsor (1981)
23. Princess Alexandra (1936)
24. James Ogilvie (1964)
25. Marina Ogilvie (1966)

Royal Residences

Audley End, Essex   Purchased by Charles II in 1669. The house had been built in 1603 to the designs of Bernard Johnson. After Charles's death, it was conveyed back to the Earl of Suffolk, as the original purchase price had never been paid in full to his ancestor. The present house is an eighteenth- and nineteenth-century remodelling of the palace.

Balmoral, Grampian   Following two visits to the Highlands, Queen Victoria and Prince Albert rented a small turreted granite castle called Balmoral, near Ballater, from 1848. In 1852 they completed the purchase of the estate. The castle was replaced by a much larger square white granite building designed by Prince Albert with assistance from William Smith of Aberdeen, son of John Smith who had designed the first castle for Sir Robert Gordon. An idea of Victoria's delight in the castle and its surroundings is conveyed by her book *Leaves from the Journal of our Life in the Highlands.* The house remains a favourite holiday residence.

Brighton Pavilion, Sussex   George IV first visited Brighton in 1783 and on land leased to him by his Clerk of the Kitchen had Henry Holland build an elegant villa similar to Holland's London house in Sloane Square. Its transformation into an Oriental fantasy was carried out by John Nash between 1815 and 1822, after which the king spent much of his time there. William IV and Queen Adelaide also used it frequently, but Victoria disliked the close contacts with the *hoi polloi* that visits to Brighton entailed. It was sold to the Town Commissioners in 1850 and is now open to the public.

Buckingham Palace, London   Built between 1702 and 1705 for John Sheffield, Duke of Buckingham, the house that took his name was designed by Captain William Winde in association with William Talman. The result, the *New View of London* reported in 1708, was 'a graceful palace . . . not to be contemned by the greatest monarch'. It was sold by Buckingham's heir in 1761 to George III who, with Queen Charlotte, took up residence in May 1762. Though royal birthdays continued to be celebrated at St James's Palace, Queen Charlotte had all but the first of her fifteen children at Buckingham Palace. After George III's death, the house's future hung in the balance as George IV lavished money on Windsor. In 1825 John Nash was summoned to rebuild and extend the Palace. He chose to recast it in York stone, and improved its setting by remodelling St James's Park, creating the lake and winding walks. William IV disliked Buckingham Palace but ordered the work to continue. The rebuilding was almost finished when he died at Windsor, making Queen Victoria the first monarch to live in the new Palace. After Prince Albert's death, the house was seldom used until the twentieth century, during which it has been the London residence of the sovereign.

Carlton House, London   A red-brick house with wings, Carlton House was built in 1709 for Henry Boyle, Lord Carlton and bought by Fredrick, Prince of Wales in 1727. Little was done to the house between the death of his widow in 1772 and the decision of the future George IV when Prince of Wales to make it his home in 1783. Henry Holland enlarged it and created some outstanding interiors. A fan-vaulted Gothic conservatory was later added by Thomas Hopper. The house was the setting for the first state visit of modern times when Tsar Alexander I was received after signing the Treaty of Paris in 1814. The house was demolished in 1827 and replaced by Carlton House Terrace overlooking St James's Park.

Clarence House, London   An extension to St James's Palace which was built for the future William IV when Duke of Clarence, Clarence House was the home of Princess Elizabeth and Prince Philip until her accession in 1952. It is now the London home of the Queen Mother.

Edinburgh Castle, Lothian   In use as a royal residence between the twelfth and late fifteenth centuries, Edinburgh Castle has been much altered over the years, only St Margaret's Chapel remaining of the earliest structures. None the less, it symbolizes the Scottish monarchy and contains the honours (regalia) of Scotland.

Eltham Palace, Kent   Many kings were familiar with Eltham Palace before it became royal property c1311 when the moated house was given to Isabella, Edward II's queen. Edward III and IV made extensive additions and it was a favoured residence during the

Above: The newly married couple *(Daily Telegraph Colour Library)*.
Opposite: The sight the crowd had been waiting for – the bride and groom returning to the Palace *(Daily Telegraph Colour Library)*.

fourteenth and fifteenth centuries. After Henry VIII met Erasmus at the Palace, it was seldom used, and by the seventeenth century was in disrepair. Little but the great hall survives.

Greenwich Palace, London   Queen Margaret, Henry VI's wife, extensively altered the earlier manor beside the Thames, and Henry VII used it as a major residence. Anne Boleyn's daughter, the future Elizabeth I, was born there, and Henry VIII enjoyed the place for its proximity to the dockyards creating the navy of which he was so proud. He also made it the home of the Royal Armouries. Tradition has it that it was at Greenwich where Sir Walter Raleigh laid his cloak on the ground for Elizabeth I. The Queen's House at Greenwich, built by Inigo Jones for Queen Anne, wife of James I, is the eldest surviving Palladian villa in England. With Anne's death in 1619 work ceased; it was not resumed until 1630, being completed for Charles I's queen, Henrietta Maria. It was at Greenwich that she had her first child; being ten weeks premature, it died within a few hours. Greenwich was nearly sold by order of the House of Commons in 1652, but it was left to Charles II to demolish the old palace and commission John Webb to build a new one. All that was built was the eastern part of the present King Charles Block of the Royal Naval Hospital. Mary II ordered Wren to adapt what had been built into the Royal Naval Hospital. When the Royal Hospital School was moved from Greenwich to Holbrook in Suffolk, the National Maritime Museum was opened in the building in 1937.

Hampton Court, Middlesex   Wolsey reputedly built this enormous palace on a site selected by eminent physicians as having the best air within 20 miles of London. Besides the house, he created gardens and a park in the surrounding 2,000 acres. Wolsey did not have long to enjoy it. Building work began only in 1515 and Wolsey had to give it to Henry VIII in 1525 in a vain bid to retain the monarch's favour. Henry enlarged it still further. The future Edward VI was born here to Jane Seymour. When James I spent Christmas at the Palace in 1601, the 1,200 rooms were not enough and tents had to be erected in the park. Charles I, Charles II and William III all spent much time at Hampton Court. Wren rebuilt the royal apartments in the late seventeenth century. George II was the last monarch to live at Hampton since George III disliked the place, partly because of the violence done to him there by his grandfather, who boxed the boy's ears. After 1760 it ceased to rank as a royal residence, and though occasional receptions are held there, many apartments are now grace and favour residences.

Hatfield House, Hertfordshire   Once the residence of the bishops of Ely and confiscated at the Reformation, Hatfield was given to Anne Boleyn's daughter Elizabeth who was reputedly sitting under an oak tree in the park when told of her accession.

James I disposed of Hatfield in 1607 by exchanging it for Theobalds in Essex with Robert Cecil, Earl of Salisbury.

Holyroodhouse, Edinburgh, Lothian Originally an abbey founded by David I, the building was converted into a royal residence by James IV. After the Earl of Surrey burned it down in 1543, it was rebuilt by James V. Charles II had it completely rebuilt, leaving only the tower house, and Prince Charles Edward Stuart gave a ball there after his victory at nearby Prestonpans (1745). It remains a royal residence for ceremonial occasions.

Kensington Palace, London The original house was built c1605 by Sir George Coppins, Clerk of the Crown. Because ministers and ambassadors grumbled about having to trek out to Hampton Court to see William and Mary, a London house proved desirable. William disliked Whitehall, so Mary's fondness for the 2nd Earl of Nottingham's house at Kensington encouraged its purchase. Wren was called upon to enlarge it, and William's provision of oil lamps along nearby Rotten Row was the first example of street lighting in England. William and Mary both died there. Queen Anne liked it as did George I who knocked down the last part of the old Nottingham House and replaced it with rooms decorated by William Kent. Work on the Serpentine to improve the house's setting was begun in the reign of George II who liked the Palace; his successor did not, allowing his brother the Duke of Kent to live there. Princess Victoria was born and grew up at Kensington Palace, and it became the residence of Princess May of Teck and currently of Princess Margaret.

Kew Palace, London A compact red-brick mansion built in 1631 by a merchant, Samuel Fortrey. George III and Queen Charlotte made what was then known as the Dutch House their residence while James Wyatt was working on a nearby Gothic palace that was never to be completed. The almost unaltered house stands in Kew Gardens.

Marlborough House, London Begun in 1709 and finished in 1711, the Duchess of Marlborough's red-brick £44,000 house was designed by Wren. It was the London home of the dukes of Marlborough until 1817 when it became the home for George IV's daughter, Princess Charlotte. It was later home to Edward, Prince of Wales, and Princess Alexandra and to George, Prince of Wales, and Princess Mary. As a widow Queen Mary returned to the house and died there in 1953. In 1959 it was transferred by the Queen to the government for use as the Commonwealth Centre.

Nonsuch, Surrey Construction of Henry VIII's vast palace of two adjoining squares began in 1538. It was granted by Mary I to the 12th Earl of Arundel in 1556. It became

Above: The famous balcony kiss *(Daily Telegraph Colour Library)*.

Below: The Duke and Duchess of York at the christening of their daughter Beatrice *(Tim Graham Picture Library)*.

Prince William and Prince Henry: second and third in the royal line of succession after their father the Prince of Wales *(Tim Graham Picture Library)*.

Elizabeth's favourite palace after she had acquired it some time between 1572 and 1592. It was there that the mud-bespattered Robert, Earl of Essex made his excuses to an unamused Elizabeth for his failure to carry out her orders in Ireland (see page 74). During the Civil War the Palace fell into disrepair, but repairs were put in hand before Charles II gave it to his celebrated mistress, the spendthrift Barbara Villiers. Always short of money, she sold it off like a twentieth-century asset stripper; by the mid-eighteenth century only the foundations were visible.

Osborne House, Isle of Wight   After purchasing the estate in 1845, Victoria and Albert erected a new house to an Italianate design by the Prince Consort. It was finished by 1851. Edward VII disliked the house and gave it to the nation in 1902, after which it became a convalescent home for officers. The House is open to the public.

Richmond Palace, Surrey   A manor house at Sheen used by Edward II and extended by Edward III, who died there, was partly demolished by Richard II. Henry V restored what was left, Henry VI enlarged it and Edward IV gave it to Elizabeth Woodville from whom Henry VII confiscated it. In 1497 fire totally destroyed it, giving Henry VII the chance to rebuild it on a grand scale, after which it was called Richmond Palace. It remained an important royal residence until the Commonwealth, after which it was stripped and sold off. Only Richmond Lodge survived, becoming home to George II as Prince of Wales and Princess Caroline, and to George II and Queen Charlotte before they moved to Kew.

St James's Palace, London   Amidst a desolate swamp beside the road from Charing Cross to Westminster stood a hospital for female lepers called the Sisters of St James in the Field. As there were only four inmates in 1532, Henry VIII felt able to give them an annuity, close the hospital and build a red-brick house with blue diaper work. He enclosed the surrounding area to form St James's Park, and took over the forest of Hyde Park, which had belonged to Westminster Abbey, enclosed it and stocked it with deer. As the principal palace for Court ceremonial, St James's was extended and embellished by Wren for James II. Critics continued to accuse it of being too unprepossessing for Court ceremonies, though even they conceded that its exterior gave no hint of the elegant interiors. After the birth of George IV, it ceased to be a royal home, though remaining the seat of sovereignty; a new monarch is proclaimed from a balcony in Friary Court, and ambassadors are still accredited to the Court of St James's.

Sandringham, Norfolk   Purchased in 1861 for Edward, Prince of Wales, who enlarged the house and developed the estate for shooting. York Cottage in the grounds was the much-loved home of George V as Prince of Wales and as monarch. Now open to the public, the house is the residence favoured by the royal family for Christmas.

Somerset House, London   Built by Jane Seymour's ill-fated brother, Edward, Duke of Somerset, the House was conveyed to Princess Elizabeth (later Elizabeth I) in exchange for Durham House in the Strand. Standing on the site of the present Somerset House, the courtyard mansion was the first major building in England to reflect the influence of the Renaissance. Elizabeth briefly took up residence here after her coronation. After the House was granted to Queen Anne (wife of James I), she largely rebuilt it and named it Denmark House after her brother, King Christian IV, stayed there in 1606. Charles I built a chapel on the tennis court for his queen, and the house was not in the list of royal houses for disposal by the Commonwealth. Oliver Cromwell's body lay in state at the House, but its fabric was in a poor state at the Restoration. It was rebuilt to plans drawn up by Wren before he died at Somerset House. Thereafter it was frequently the royal dower-house. In 1775 Somerset House was handed over to the government in exchange for Buckingham Palace; Sir William Chambers rebuilt it for government use in the form that can be seen today.

Stirling Castle, Central   A fort of kinds stood on the impregnable volcanic outcrop at Stirling from the eleventh century. It became a royal residence in the following century, Alexander I staying there. What remains dates from the fifteenth century and later, of which the magnificent great hall built by Robert Cochrane is noteworthy. Involved in the recurrent warfare between England and Scotland, the Castle was a garrison until 1964.

Theobalds, Hertfordshire   James I acquired Theobalds by exchanging it for Hatfield House with Robert Cecil, Earl of Salisbury, in 1607. It became his favourite residence and he died there in 1625. Parliament ordered its sale in 1650 and it was gradually dismantled.

Tower of London   William I incorporated Roman walls in his castle to hold the capital. Successive rulers strengthened its fortifications, particularly the addition of the White Tower, completed c1100, to protect the armoury, mint, royal Treasury and wardrobe, where the Crown jewels are kept. Henry VIII was the last king to use it as a chief residence.

Palace of Westminster, London   The building history of the principal residence of English kings from Edward the Confessor to Henry VIII is complex. Much has been lost through fires and insensitive demolition during Victorian times, particularly the thirteenth-century Painted Chamber which was destroyed to make way for Barry's present Houses of Parliament. Since Henry's move to Whitehall, it has gradually become the meeting place for the Houses of Parliament and the site of government offices.

Whitehall Palace, London   Originally known as York Place and handed over by Wolsey to Henry VIII, along with Hampton Court, Whitehall's change of name is referred to in Shakespeare's *Henry VIII*. Henry enlarged it with materials from Kensington Palace and Esher Palace, and James I built a Banqueting Hall which was destroyed by fire through the carelessness of workmen setting fire to 'oily clothes' used in a masque. Inigo Jones replaced it with the present Hall, decorated by Rubens for Charles I and the only part of the old Palace to survive following a devastating fire in 1798. Government offices were built on the site.

Windsor Castle, Berkshire   Originally a motte and two baileys built by William I in 1067, Windsor was developed by successive monarchs to become the main royal residence. Henry I first used stone and is thought to have built the shell keep on the motte, and Henry II made extensive additions. By the end of Edward III's reign, the Castle had ceased to be primarily a military stronghold (it had been besieged unsuccessfully in 1194 and 1216) and became first and foremost a residence. Edward III created St George's Hall and founded the Order of the Garter. Edward IV began the Garter chapel of St George, and the most significant improvements and additions were thereafter made by Charles II, George III and George IV, who rebuilt much of the Castle.

Woodstock, Oxfordshire   Set in a royal forest, Woodstock was a pre-Conquest retreat for English kings. Henry I created a royal menagerie there, and for Henry II it competed with Clarendon (Wiltshire) as his favourite country residence, associated with his mistress Rosamund. Henry III was nearly murdered there, after which security at all royal palaces was tightened. By the sixteenth century the Palace was dilapidated, though it held out for twenty days during a Civil War siege. In 1705 the estate was given to the Duke of Marlborough for his service during the War of Spanish Succession and the last fragments of the old Palace were removed c1718.

Winchester Palace, Hampshire   Winchester was the principal royal residence and seat of government of both the Anglo-Saxon and Norman kings, and the site of the Anglo-Saxon kings' mausoleum. The Domesday Book was kept in the Castle. In Henry II's reign the Exchequer and Treasury were transferred to Westminster. The various stages of building were repeatedly damaged by fire or siege (1141), and after the royal chambers were destroyed in 1302, they were never fully rebuilt. The Bishop's Palace became the residence for kings staying in the city. The great hall of Henry III – with its Arthurian associations through the great round table – remains, but the Castle was dismantled in 1651. A palace designed by Wren for Charles II was never completed and was adapted to become a barracks.

Members of the royal family watching the Trooping the Colour from the balcony of
Buckingham Palace *(Tim Graham Picture Library)*.

FACTS AND DATES

European Monarchy in the Twentieth Century

When Queen Victoria died in 1901, England was one of about twenty European
monarchies. In the second half of the twentieth century, only ten remain: Britain
(Windsor); Denmark and Norway (with the common surname Schleswig-Holstein-
Sonderburg-Glücksburg); Sweden (Bernadotte); Belgium (Saxe-Coburg-Gotha);
Holland (Orange); Luxembourg (Orange); Monaco (Grimaldi); Liechtenstein
(Brandis); and Spain (monarchy reinstituted on the death of General Franco in 1975).

Portugal was the first country to lose its dynasty, the Braganzas, in 1910. During and
immediately after World War I the Romanovs (Russia), the Hohenzollerns (Germany),
the Habsburgs (Austria), and the ruling house of Montenegro were overthrown.

Between the world wars Turkey (Ottoman) and Spain (Bourbon) became republics,
as did Greece from 1923 to 1935, and again from 1973. The monarchies of Romania,
Yugoslavia and Bulgaria disappeared during World War II. Italy (Savoy) and Albania
became republics in 1946.

Commonwealth Countries

There are 48 member countries of the Commonwealth. Queen Elizabeth is Head of State of 18; there are 26 republics and 5 are monarchies with other sovereigns. The Queen is symbolic Head of the Commonwealth.

The Queen's Realm
Antigua and Barbuda, Australia, Bahamas, Barbados, Belize, Britain, Canada, Fiji, Grenada, Jamaica, Mauritius, New Zealand, Papua New Guinea, St Christopher and Nevis, St Lucia, St Vincent and the Grenadines, Solomon Islands and Tuvalu.

Republics
Bangladesh, Botswana, Cyprus, Dominica, The Gambia, Ghana, Guyana, India, Kenya, Kiribati, Malawi, Maldives, Nauru, Nigeria, Pakistan, Seychelles, Sierra Leone, Singapore, Sri Lanka, Tanzania, Trinidad and Tobago, Uganda, Vanuatu, Western Samoa, Zambia, Zimbabwe.

Other Monarchies
Brunei, Lesotho, Malaysia, Swaziland, Tonga.

Prime Ministers 1830–1989

1830 Earl Grey (Lib)
1834 Lord Melbourne (Lib)
1834 Sir Robert Peel (Con)
1835 Lord Melbourne (Lib)
1841 Sir Robert Peel (Con)
1846 Lord John Russell (Lib)
1852 Earl of Derby (Con)
1852 Earl of Aberdeen (Lib-Coalition)
1855 Lord Palmerston (Lib)
1865 Earl Russell (Lib)
1866 Earl of Derby (Con)
1868 Benjamin Disraeli (Con)
1868 William Gladstone (Lib)
1874 Benjamin Disraeli (Con)
1880 William Gladstone (Lib)
1885 Marquess of Salisbury (Con)
1886 William Gladstone (Lib)

1886 Marquess of Salisbury (Con-Unionist)
1892 William Gladstone (Lib)
1894 Earl of Rosebery (Lib)
1895 Marquess of Salisbury (Con-Unionist)
1902 A. J. Balfour (Con-Unionist)
1905 Sir Henry Campbell-Bannerman (Lib)
1908 H. H. Asquith (Lib)
1915 H. H. Asquith (Coalition)
1916 D. Lloyd George (Coalition)
1922 A. Bonar Law (Con)
1923 Stanley Baldwin (Con)
1924 J. Ramsay Macdonald (Lab)
1924 Stanley Baldwin (Con)
1929 J. Ramsay Macdonald (Lab)

1931 J. Ramsay Macdonald (National)

1935 Stanley Baldwin (National)

1937 Neville Chamberlain (National)

1940 Winston Churchill (Coalition)

1945 C. R. Attlee (Lab)

1951 Winston Churchill (Con)

1955 Sir Anthony Eden (Con)

1957 Harold Macmillan (Con)

1963 Sir Alec Douglas-Home (Con)

1964 Harold Wilson (Lab)

1966 Harold Wilson (Lab)

1970 Edward Heath (Con)

1974 Harold Wilson (Lab)

1974 Harold Wilson (Lab)

1976 James Callaghan (Lab)

1979 Margaret Thatcher (Con)

1983 Margaret Thatcher (Con)

1987 Margaret Thatcher (Con)

Palmerston became Prime Minister at the age of 71. Disraeli was aged 69 in his second term of office. Gladstone formed governments when aged 71, 75 and 83. Campbell-Bannerman formed his first government when he was 69. Churchill was 75 when he led the Conservatives to victory in 1951, and was Prime Minister again in his 80th year.

British Wars and Campaigns 1775–1945

With U.S.A. 1775–1782

With France 1778–1783

With Spain 1780–1783

With Netherlands 1780–1782

With France 1793–1802

With Napoleon 1803–1815

With U.S.A. 1812–1814

With Russia (Crimean War) 1854–1856

Indian Mutiny 1857–1858

With Abyssinia 1868

With Ashanti 1873–1874

With Afghanistan 1878–1880

With Zulus 1879

With Egypt 1882

With Sudanese 1881–1898

First Boer War 1880–1882

Boxer Rising 1896–1900

Second Boer War 1899–1902

First World War 1914–1918

Second World War 1939–1945

Major British Army Operational Deployments 1945–1990

Palestine 1945–1948

Aden 1947, 1958, 1964–1967

Malaya 1948–1960

Korean War 1950–1958

Kenya 1952–1956

Suez 1956

Brunei 1962

Borneo 1963–1966

Northern Ireland 1969–

Falklands War 1982

Beirut (UN) 1983

Namibia (UN) 1989

World War I 1914–1918

By 1907, Europe was divided into two armed camps: the Triple Alliance of Germany, Austria and Italy versus the Triple Entente of Britain, France and Russia. Between 1908 and 1913, a series of events in the Balkans and North Africa, reflecting nascent nationalism and international rivalries, brought Europe to the verge of war.

On 28 June 1914 the heir to the throne of Austria-Hungary, Archduke Franz Ferdinand, was assassinated at Sarajevo. Very soon only Italy and Britain remained aloof from the general European War. Britain strove to confine the war to the Balkans, but after German violation of Belgian neutrality was brought into the struggle on 4 August 1914. Italy joined in on the side of the Allies in 1915.

Britain's main contribution was on the Western Front, in France and Belgium. In 1914, and throughout 1915, the BEF, under the command of Sir John French, stabilized the Allied line southwards from the Channel ports with very heavy losses, particularly at Ypres and Loos. At this stage Sir Douglas Haig replaced French. An attempt to distract attention from the Western Front by making a landing on the Gallipoli peninsula in the Dardanelles, was a disastrous and costly failure (1915). An Allied offensive along the Somme in 1916 gained a mere seven miles at a cost to Britain alone of 420,000 casualties.

There were few naval actions. A minor German success at Coronel, off Chile, in 1914 was quickly avenged at the battle of the Falkland Islands. In May 1916 a major fleet action took place at the Battle of Jutland. It ended indecisively and was followed by a German submarine offensive against Allied and neutral shipping.

In April 1917 the United States entered the war. This addition of manpower, and the Allied blockade of Germany, meant that the end was in sight. The German High Command withdrew twenty-five miles to the Siegfried, or Hindenburg, line to make Allied offensives more difficult – the Passchendaele offensive (1917) cost 300,000 British lives.

In 1918 the Germans threw all their resources into attacks which seriously undermined their already weak position. From September onwards the German army was on the point of defeat, whilst the civilian population was on the verge of starvation. The Armistice was signed on the morning of 11 November 1918, and ended the war in which three-quarters of a million British soldiers had died.

The peace treaty with Germany was concluded at Versailles (1919). The Allied signatories were Lloyd George (Britain); Clemenceau (France); Woodrow Wilson (America); and Orlando (Italy). Germany, which had not been a party to the negotiations, was saddled with an astronomical war indemnity, deprived of most of her coal, iron and steel, and separated from her possessions in Eastern Europe. The seeds of World War II were sown by the peacemakers after World War I.

World War II 1939–1945

The principal cause of the war was Hitler's aggressive and expansionist policy, typified by the seizure of Austria, Czechoslovakia and Poland. Britain and France declared war on Germany on 3 September 1939, after German entry into Poland on 1 September. The Commonwealth countries followed Great Britain's example.

Germany invaded Norway, Denmark, Belgium and Holland; and Russia (bound to Germany in 1939) invaded Finland. The British Expeditionary Force in France found itself cut off and surrounded, and withdrew to Dunkirk, where evacuation took place in May 1940. Italy now entered the war on Germany's behalf; the Germans entered Paris, and Britain was left alone against the Axis Powers.

In the late summer and autumn of 1940, the Battle of Britain was fought in the air and Britain saved from invasion. In 1941, Hitler invaded Russia and turned an ally into an enemy. Japan attacked Pearl Harbour and brought the United States into the war, which now became world-wide.

The year 1942 was the turning-point. On land, at sea and in the air, the initiative gradually passed to the Allies. Montgomery and Eisenhower cleared the Germans out of North Africa, the prelude to the invasion of Sicily in 1943. At sea, radar and carrier-based planes were effectively combating the menace of German U-boats. Allied bombing raids ruined the productive capacity of the Ruhr.

The Allied invasion of Sicily in 1943 caused the downfall of Mussolini (July) and led to the Italian Armistice on 3 September. The conquest of German-occupied Italy began. In the Far East (1943), naval battles stemmed the Japanese advance in the Pacific and were followed by American landings on Pacific islands. British and Commonwealth forces halted the Japanese advance in Burma.

Allied landings in Normandy in 1944 resulted in the liberation of France and Belgium. The Allies entered Rome in June 1944. The Russians resumed the offensive on the Eastern Front, in Poland, the Baltic and the Balkans.

In March 1945, the Allies crossed the Rhine. Hitler's death was announced in May, shortly before the Russians entered Berlin. On 9 May the Germans agreed to unconditional surrender. On 12 September, following atom-bomb attacks on Hiroshima and Nagasaki, the Japanese surrendered.

GLOSSARY

advowson	right of presentation of a benefice
bailey	courtyard within walls of castle
Covenant	manifesto of those opposed to Charles I's religious policies in Scotland
episcopacy	government of Church by bishops
fief	sphere of control
fyrd	Anglo-Saxon term for local military force in which all free men were obliged to serve
heir apparent	one whose right of inheritance cannot be superseded by birth of another
heir presumptive	one whose right of inheritance can be superseded by birth of another
motte	earth mounds on which fortification erected
poll tax	a tax, first introduced in 1222, on every individual over 14 years of age. From Middle High German *polle*. Provoked Peasant's Revolt
praemunire	powers and privileges belonging to sovereign
see	episcopal unit
ship money	tax first levied on coastal town to fund navy, later extended inland
thegn	Anglo-Saxon noble holding estates in return for service
villein	medieval peasant
Witan	Anglo-Saxon council called to give advice to king. Helped prevent autocracy

BIBLIOGRAPHY

Ashley, Morris. *England in the Seventeenth Century* (Penguin, 1952)

Cannon, John and Griffiths, Ralph. *The Oxford Illustrated History of the British Monarchy* (OUP, 1988)

Faulkus, Malcolm and Gillingham, John (eds). *Historical Atlas of Britain* (Grisewood & Dempsey, 1981)

Fulford, Roger. *Hanover to Windsor* (Batsford, 1960)

Hedley, Olwen. *Royal Palaces* (Hale, 1972)

Kenyon, J. P. (ed). *A Dictionary of British History* (Secker & Warburg, 1981)

Kenyon, J. P. *The Stuarts* (Batsford, 1958)

Lambert, Anthony J. *Victorian and Edwardian Country-House Life* (Batsford, 1981)

Lockyer, Roger. *Tudor and Stuart Britain, 1471–1714* (Longman, 1964)

Lofts, Norah. *Queens of Britain* (Hodder & Stoughton, 1977)

Magnus, Philip. *Edward VII* (Murray, 1964)

Morris, Christopher. *The Tudors* (Batsford, 1955)

Plumb, J. H. *England in the Eighteenth Century* (Penguin, 1950)

Plumb, J. H. *The First Four Georges* (Batsford, 1956)

Rose, Kenneth. *Kings, Queens & Courtiers* (Weidenfeld and Nicolson, 1985)

Somerset Fry, Plantagenet. *The David & Charles Book of Castles* (David & Charles, 1980)

Sproule, Anna. *Lost Houses of Britain* (David & Charles, 1982)

Thorne, J. O. and Collocott, T. C. (eds). *Chambers Biographical Dictionary* (Chambers, 1984)

Trevelyan, G. M. *History of England* (Longman, 1926)

Trevelyan, G. M. *English Social History* (Longman, 1944)

Williamson, David. *Kings and Queens of Britain* (Webb & Bower/Michael Joseph, 1986)

INDEX

Page numbers in italics denote illustrations

The BRITISH ISLES

N

SCOTLAND

Highland

Grampian

Tayside

Fife

Central

Lothian

Strathclyde

Borders

Dumfries
and
Galloway

Northumberland

Tyne and Wear

Western Isles

Northern Ireland

Londonderry